CONTENTS

DEDICATION

First and foremost, I can't thank my wife Leanne enough, who over the years has put up with me having fishing gear throughout the house, going on holidays where I just have to get a couple of days fishing in, to coming home smelling like a fish. I could not have achieved over the past 40 years without your devotion and help, and you thought that you were marrying a surfer.

To my kids Chris and Alissa and the times that you have put up with me wanting to have that one more cast. To the times when I have made you hold up a fish even though you didn't want to.

I will always remember when I took Chris for his first ever offshore fishing trip through the breakers off Gerroa Beach and how over the next 3-years we won the open teams' event three years in a row for the Gerroa Boat Fisherman's Fishing Club.

To the day that I took out Alissa and Andrew for her first real go at targeting dusky flathead with soft plastics only to have Alissa smash Andrew with her PB of 79cm and then not want to hold onto it for a photo, so I had to get into the shot.

When I first met Andrew (favourite son-in-law) he didn't have much an interest in fishing, but over the years this has changed. Alissa reckons that I have brainwashed him into liking fishing. I don't see a problem with that and one of our many trips that comes to mind was when Andrew, Dennis and I drove to Port Phillip bay in a day, fished for the next two days and drove back on the fourth day.

Outside of my family I have had so many people that have influenced my way of fishing.

David Tosland who has put up with my ups and downs over the past 12 years fishing a variety of fishing tournaments from the Gold Coast Flathead Classic to Bream Tournaments as far down as Mallacoota in Victoria with me from when we have won events to when we have come last. The learning experience has been tremendous.

Scotty Lyons who owns and operates Southern Sydney Fishing Tours and is the "Hook" part of the Hook and Cook You Tube Channel. Many a time I have fished with Scotty and his dad Bill from off the rocks, in the estuary and offshore. Scott and Bill have taught me so much over the years and they too are great anglers in their own right.

Currently I am sponsored by Tackle Tactics whose gear I have been using for years now and I am not just saying it, I can't fault it. Over the years Gareth, Justin and the rest of the crew and Pro Anglers have put so much effort into testing their range of gear that it keeps on getting better and better.

If you get a chance you need to check out their extremely informative web page at **http://tackletactics. com.au/Home-Page** where they have TT Lures, Zman, Pro Cure Scent, Okuma, Platypus lines, Fish Inc Lures, Mepps and Bagley lures. Just to name a few.

Last and by no means least is Bill Classon from AFN for the faith in allowing me to put together my first edition of the Fishing Guide to Sydney-Hawkesbury back in 2002 which has led to me scribing another 4 books, revisions, feature articles and hopefully a few more books to come.

First published 2024

Published and distributed by
AFN Fishing & Outdoors
PO Box 544 Croydon, Victoria 3136
Telephone: (03) 9729 8788
Email: sales@afn.com.au   www.afn.com.au

©Australian Fishing Network 2024

ISBN: 9781 8651 3426 0

Printed in China

The book will help those anglers who do not own a boat or who cannot get out on the water with a mate to fish the areas on Botany Bay, the Georges, Woronora and the Port Hacking Rivers in Southern Sydney.

As you work your way through the 60 land-based spots that I have selected you will be given an insight into what type of place it is, the targeted species that you can catch there, the best months to target them and what techniques to use.

I will also give you some of the suggested baits and lures that I have successfully used over the years. Plus, when are the best times and tides.

The bulk of these spots are very easy to find, but just in case you get lost I will also be letting you know how to get there and what you can expect to find in the way of amenities and what there is to do with family and friends, other than fishing.

SAFETY MESSAGE

Consideration for others and always think of safety first. No fish is worth your life.

You may not think that fishing from the shore can be dangerous, but it can. It doesn't take much to trip and fall while going down a set of stairs or track to a new found fishing spot. So care needs to be taken at all times. Wear the correct footwear, take a torch during your nighttime sojourns and don't be in such a rush.

In this book there are a number of places where you have to park near private residences. Make sure that you treat them with respect, don't make unnecessary noise and never leave your garbage behind.

When fishing off the ocean rocks you will need to keep an eye on the swell. It would be a good idea to never fish alone and always wear a life jacket. Once again wearing the correct footwear is essential. Even though fishing off the beach seems very safe you will need to keep an eye on those shifting sand bars.

Back in the late fifties Gary Brown started fishing the George's River and Botany Bay for bream, flathead, luderick, flounder, and whiting, then progressing to the Port Hacking and Woronora Rivers, adding leatherjackets, crabs, tailor, mullet, black bream, estuary perch, snapper and mulloway to the list.

While travelling to Queensland for his annual holidays with his dad and mum, they would stop off at a number of places so that they could fish their way up to Brisbane. The return trip would be the same as the one going up. Fish as many places as the time would allow.

Gary has also been fishing off the beaches since he was 10 and the rocks since he was 14 and over the years has travelled extensively around the coastline of Australia fishing in both very populated and remote areas. In those early years most of his beach and rock fishing was concentrated from Palm Beach in Sydney and down to Seven Mile Beach at Gerroa we he used to live.

It was when Gary turned 21, he felt the urge to explore many other beaches and rocks that can be found around Australia. In 1975 he found myself in Western Australia fishing beaches and rock platforms from Yanchep, just north of Perth and south to Margaret River with a mate of his. While over in the west Gary also fished some of the remote beaches from Cape Freycinet to Albany. On his way back to the east coast of Australia he fished at places like Ceduna, Portland, Barwon Heads, Wilson's Promontory and Mallacoota.

Throughout his school and working years he continued to fish venues throughout New South Wales, and then interstate to Victoria, South Australia, Tasmania, Queensland and Western Australia.

Gary now lives back in the Sutherland Shire and while continuing to fish, he has developed, written and taught a course on recreational fishing for TAFE, started up fishing classes in various tackle and boating shops throughout Sydney. Gary also writes for a number of online fishing and boating site and one that he is very proud of is that he is still writing for NSWFM after starting his first column back in October 1996. He has never missed a month.

Gary has also written and or co-written 5 more books for AFN. They are:

• Fishing Atlas to Sydney-Hawkesbury. Revised 2020.

• How to fish the Beaches and Rocks of Australia. 2005.

• Fishing guide to south of Sydney. 2010

• How to catch Australia's favourite saltwater fish. 2011.

• Land based fishing guide to the Sydney Area. 2013.

He has also put together a couple of dvd's with Scotty Lyons from Southern Sydney Fishing Tours called "A Day on the Bay" and "The Jewel of the South".

Over the past number of years Gary has expanded his knowledge of fishing and boating by competing in a number of bream and flathead tournaments up and down the east coast of Australia.

Follow Gary on Instagram at **gary1079 or email gbrown1@iprimus.com.au**

Gary Brown

UPPER GEORGES RIVER

BANKSI

BEXLEY NORTH

BEVERLY HILLS

KOGARAH

HURSTVILLE

ALLAWAH

REVESBY HEIGHTS

LUGARNO

OATLEY

GEORGES RIVER

KOGARAH BAY

SANDRINGHAM

GEORGES RIVER

Kyle Bay

Coronation Bay

Oyster Bay

Captain Cook Bridge

COMO

BONNET BAY

MIRANDA

WOOLWARE BAY

WORONORA HEIGHTS

SUTHERLAND

YARRAWARRAH

GYMEA BAY

YOWIE BAY

CRONU

CARINGBAH SOUTH

GRAYS POINT

LILLI PILLI

BURRANEER

WARUMBUL

PORT HACKING

MAIANBAR

BUN

South West Pt.

SYDNEY AIRPORT

BOTANY

NO BOATS OR FISHING ALLOWED

BOTANY BAY

Brotherson Dock. No Boating Allowed

MATRAVILLE

PORT BOTANY

Yarra Bay

FUGE ZONE

WEENEY BAY

QUIBRAY BAY

KURNELL

BATE BAY

ILLS H

1. MAROUBRA BEACH – *page 00*
2. LONG BAY
3. BARE ISLAND
4. LA PEROUSE
5. FRENCHMAN'S BAY
6. YARRA BAY SAILING CLUB
7. COOK RIVER BREAKWALL
8. THE GRAND PARADE BRIGHTON

9. RAMSGATE BATHS
10. DOLLS POINT
11. GEORGES RIVER 16FT SAILING CLUB
12. BONNA POINT/SLIVER BEACH
13. SUTHERLAND POINT – BOTANY BAY NATIONAL PARK
14. CAPTIAN COOK BRIDGE
15. THE PROMONARDE-KOGARAH BAY
16. CARSS PARK BATHS
17. TOM UGLY'S BRIDGE
18. BALD FACE POINT
19. OATLEY BAY BOAT RAMP
20. OATLEY POINT
21. COMO PLEASURE GROUNDS-COMO BRIDGE
22. OATLEY PARK BATHS

23. LUGARNO WALKWAY
24. OLD FERRY ROAD ILLAWONG
25. GEORGE RIVER STATE NATIONAL PARK
26. KELSO BEACH RESERVE
27. MILPERA BRIDGE
28. LAKEWOOD CITY RESERVE-WORONORA
29. JANNALI RESERVE BOAT RAMP
30. THE OLD WORONORA RIVER BRIDGE/WEST
31. THE OLD WORONORA RIVER BRIDGE/EAST
32. PRINCE EDWARD PARK – WORONORA RIVER
33. MULLET ROCK
34. BOAT HARBOUR
35. GREEN HILLS
36. WANDA BEACH
37. CRONULLA POINT
38. WINDY POINT
39. DAROOK PARK
40. GUNNAMATTA BAY BATHS
41. TONKIN PARK
42. WATER STREET RAMP
43. DOYLANS BAY BOAT RAMP
44. LILLY PILLY BATHS
45. YOWIE BAY BOAT RAMP
46. GYMEA BAY BATHS
47. GRAYS POINT FLATS
48. SWALLOW ROCK DRIVE RESERVE
49. REIDS FLAT-ROYAL NATIONAL PARK
50. POOL FLAT – ROYAL NATIONAL PARK
51. WARUMBUL ROAD PICNIC AREA
52. COSTENS POINT TRAIL
53. MAINIBAR
54. DEE BAN SPIT
55. CABBAGE TREE BASIN
56. BUNDEENA
57. BUNDEENA POINT
58. JIBBON BEACH
59. JIBBON POINT
60. WATTAMOLLA BEACH

MAROUBRA BEACH

🔍 HOW TO GET THERE

Travel east along Maroubra Road until you reach Malabar Road. Vere off slightly to continue along Maroubra Road until you reach Arthur Byrne Reserve. Here you will find parking and it's just a short walk to the beach.

🔍 SNAPSHOT

PLATFORM
BEACH

TARGET FISH
BREAM
SAND WHITING
SILVER TREVALLY
SALMON
TAILOR
DART

BEST BAIT
BLOOD WORMS
PINK NIPPERS
WHOLE & HALF PILCHARDS
WHITEBAIT
STRIPS OF MULLET

BEST LURES
METAL SLICES
SOFT PLASTICS
SOFT VIBES

BEST TIMES
EARLY MORNING
& LATE AFTERNOON
ON A FALLING TIDE

SEASONS

Bream **February to May**

Dart
Year round

Sand whiting
October to April

Silver trevally
March to June

Salmon **March to June**

Tailor **March to August**

When patrolling Maroubra Beach keep a look out for those gutters. Even if they are small, they will still produce a few fish.

When the surf is not too big you can try using a 2.1m rod with a small running ball sinker down onto the hook and a beach worm for bait. Just like Riley Brown has.

Maroubra beach is a very popular surfing location in Sydney. It has two surf life-saving clubs and is patrolled all year by Randwick City lifeguards. Care will need to be taken when fishing here as you don't want to hook and surfer or swimmer.

It's popular with visitors given its easy access and large kilometre-long expanse of sand and at the northern end you will find a rocky headland. Arthur Byrne Reserve and headland are to the south, and Broadarrow Reserve is to the west.

TACTICS

As with all beaches you will find that the gutters will come and go, but most of the year you will find some kind of gutter on the northern and southern ends of the beach. As you will see there is a rocky formation towards the northern end of the beach. Try using either a single or double paternoster rig here when the seas are up a bit. During the calmer seas, you could revert back to the sinker down onto the swivel and have a leader of about 50 to 75cm. When casting out your rig try to land it near the edges of the sand bank where the water is flowing into the deeper water.

BAITS AND LURES

Bream, whiting, trevally and dart prefer either beach or blood worms, pipis and small pieces of pilchards. You could also try using small whitebait, mullet and tuna for the bream.

Even though salmon and tailor will take the above baits, I would try using whole pilchards and garfish on a set of ganged hooks. 40 to 80-gram metal slicers are always handy to have on hand, as you can get more distance when the fish are out wide.

BEST TIDE/TIMES

Due to the popularity of the beach I would concentrate my fishing time to early mornings or late afternoons. Days when it's a bit wet are also great times to have a fish. A couple of hours either side of the bottom or top of the tide seems to produce more bites.

When fishing the gutters adjacent to the rocks you should concentrate you time for fishing to the run-out tide.

AMENITIES

There are outdoor showers, a large changeroom and toilet and lighting. There is also a cafe/kiosk area at the centre of the beach and more restaurants and cafes are located in Marine Parade directly opposite the beach.

KIDS AND FAMILIES

There's lots to do at the beach with a free outdoor gym, a skate park and a large kid's playground. Free BBQs are located in the central part of the beach and towards the south of the beach near South Maroubra Surf Club.

There is free parking surrounding the beach, including a car park adjacent to the main beach, a car park north of the beach at Jack Vanny Reserve and a car park at South Maroubra Beach.

LONG BAY

HOW TO GET THERE

Turn into Franklin Street off Anzac Parade. Then turn right into Dacre Street, then right into Fisherman's Road. Parking is fairly limited, so you may have to park in an adjoining street and then walk a short distance to the beach or rocks.

Trevally, bream and tailor can be caught here. Just remember to fish as light as possible and berley.

SNAPSHOT

PLATFORM
OCEAN ROCK
SMALL BEACH

TARGET FISH
BREAM
DRUMMER
GARFISH
LUDERICK
MULLET
SILVER TREVALLY
SQUID

BEST BAIT
WHOLE & HALF PILCHARDS
GARFISH
SQUID, PRAWNS
CABBAGE
GREEN WEED
SALMON

BEST LURES
METAL LURES
STICK BAITS
SURFACE LURES

BEST TIMES
FISH WHEN SWELL IS
SMALL, FALLING TIDE

SEASONS
Bream
February to May
Drummer
March to August
Garfish
Year round
Luderick
March to August
Mullet
Year round
Silver trevally
March to June
Squid
Year round

ABOVE: *Luderick frequent this spot and can be caught while suspending green weed or cabbage below an A-Just-a-Bubble float.*

Malabar Beach is situated in the corner of Long Bay and is one of Randwick City's lesser-known beaches. There is a rock pool located on the southern foreshore below Randwick Golf Club. On the northern side of the bay is a boat ramp and the home base for the Randwick District Offshore Rescue Boat.

Long Bay is an IPAs and the collecting of seashore animals is strictly prohibited in these closures. This includes crabs, snails, cunjevoi, octopus, sea urchins, anemones, pipis, cockles, mussels, oysters, and nippers. The area extends from the mean high-water mark to 10 metres seaward from the mean low water mark. Fishing is permitted in these areas, but bait collection is not allowed, although you may bring bait with you up to the quantity allowed by NSW Fisheries.

TACTICS

Due to the snaggy bottom, it would be best if you fish with either a small bobby cork or a stem float. As this will keep your bait off the bottom. You could also try using a small (000, 00) ball sinker directly down onto the bait. Making sure that you stay in contact with the bait at all times.

When the seas are up and the swell comes into this small bay you will find that the tailor and salmon sometime move in. Either use a larger bobby cork and suspend a whole pilchard or garfish underneath. You could also try using a lightly weighted pilchard or garfish on a set of ganged hooks.

BAITS AND LURES

Pink nippers, peeled prawns, pudding baits, pillie tails or strips of mullet and tuna. Whole pilchards and garfish for the tailor and salmon. 40 to 80-gram metal slicers are always handy to have on hand, as you can get more distance when the fish are out wide.

BEST TIDE/TIMES

Due to the bay being shallow I would concentrate your fishing tide to about two hours either side of the top of the tide.

AMENITIES

Cromwell Park is located directly behind the beach where there is a children's playground and public toilets, showers and changerooms.

KIDS AND FAMILIES

The beach is popular with families due to the normally placid conditions. Walking, jogging, sunbathing, snorkelling, scuba diving and kayaking are all popular activities.

There are two shipwrecks in the bay, the MV Malabar and the Goolgwai, both popular with divers.

BARE ISLAND

🔍 HOW TO GET THERE

When coming in from the west you can travel east along Botany Road. Turn left into Bunnerong Road and then follows this down to the end of Anzac Parade. Parking here can be hard at times and you may have to park in a side street.

🔍 SNAPSHOT

Platform
OCEAN ROCK

Target species
BREAM
BONITO
DRUMMER
DUSKY FLATHEAD
KINGFISH
LUDERICK
PANED SNAPPER
SALMON
SAND WHITING
SILVER TREVALLY
SQUID
TAILOR
YELLOWTAIL

Best bait
WHOLE & HALF PILCHARDS
GARFISH, SQUID,
PRAWNS, CABBAGE
GREEN WEED

Best lures
METAL SLICERS
STICK BAITS
SURFACE LURES

Best time
VERY SMALL SWELL,
FALLING TIDE

SEASONS
Bream **February to May**
Bonito **November to May**
Drummer **March to August**
Dusky Flathead
November to April
Kingfish **February to May**
Luderick **March to September**
Paned sized napper **Winter**
Salmon **March to June**
Sand Whiting **October to April**
Silver Trevally
March to June
Squid **Year round**
Tailor **March to August**
Yellowtail **Year round**

Take a walk across the bridge to Bare Island where you can target bream, trevally and luderick.

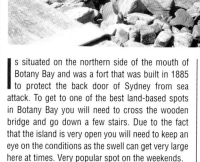

Is situated on the northern side of the mouth of Botany Bay and was a fort that was built in 1885 to protect the back door of Sydney from sea attack. To get to one of the best land-based spots in Botany Bay you will need to cross the wooden bridge and go down a few stairs. Due to the fact that the island is very open you will need to keep an eye on the conditions as the swell can get very large here at times. Very popular spot on the weekends.

TACTICS
Once there you will see that the surrounding rock areas of the island is very close to the water. Care will need to be taken here when fishing. Rock shoes are a must. If the seas are very big you can fish off the bridge or the rocks on the northern side of the island.
Try suspending a whole pilchard or garfish under a bobby cork, as the water is very deep on the NE side of the island. Use a lightly weighted bait to fish the number of washes that are found here.
Don't forget to take along a few metal slicers for the salmon and tailor that frequent this area. Drummer and luderick are best fish for when using a flat or a small bobby cork. Make sure that you berley well to keep the fish in the area you are fishing.

BAITS AND LURES
Pilchards, garfish, mullet, prawns, cunje, green weed, cabbage, tuna and bread are the go here.

ABOVE: *Luderick are a common sort after species off Bare Island. Remember it's now law to wear a life jacket when fishing from here.*

You could also try suspending a yellowtail, squid or slimy mackerel under a bobby cork.
Surface lures like the Fish Inc 120mm Wing and 160mm Hooker stick baits or the 140mm Fish Inc Scrum Half popper would be great for bonito and kingfish. As for soft plastics, you could try the ZMAN 7-inch scented Jerk Shadz on 5/0 to 7/0 TT jig heads.

BEST TIDE/TIMES
Now this will depend on what fish species you are going to target. All of the fish species that are listed will feed on both the run-in and run-out tides.

AMENITIES
Toilets, drinking water and a nearby restaurant and kiosk.

KIDS AND FAMILIES
Playground for the kids is nearby. There are a number of nearby walking tracks that will take you out to Henry Head and the Botany Bay National Park. While there on a Sunday you make like to take a tour (fee) of the Bare Island Fort.
Sometimes a local reptile handler will set up in the park nearby and give demonstration on his reptiles.

HOW TO GET THERE 🔍

When coming in from the west you can travel east along Botany Road. Turn left into Bunnerong Road and then follows this down to the end of Anzac Parade. Parking here can be hard at times and you may have to park in a side street.

Parking maybe a problem here at times, but getting into a couple of fish is just a matter of casting a line.

LEFT: *Parking can be a problem here, but it's worth find some. As the fishing can be very good here. Remember you must wear a life jacket when fishing from here.*

SNAPSHOT 🔍

Platform
ROCK PLATFORM
SMALL BEACH

Target species
BREAM, DUSKY
FLATHEAD
FLOUNDER
SALMON
SAND WHITING
SILVER TREVALLY
SQUID AND TAILOR

Best baits
WHOLE & HALF PILCHARDS
GARFISH, SQUID
PRAWNS, CABBAGE
GREEN WEED
RED /BROWN CRABS

Best lures
METAL SLICES
STICK BAITS
SURFACE LURES

Best time
PROTECTED ROCK PLATFORM
FALLING TIDE

SEASONS

Bream **February to May**

Dusky flathead **November to April**

Flounder **November to April**

Salmon **March to June**

Sand whiting **October to April**

Silver trevally & salmon **March to June**

Squid **Year round**

Tailor **March to August**

There is a small point that is located just inside Bare Island that is a great place to cast a line out onto a sandy bottom. Surface fish like tailor, salmon and the odd bonito do school up here at times. During the weekend this point can get very crowded.

TACTICS

Once there you will see that the surrounding rock areas of the island is very close to the water. Care will need to be taken here when fishing. Rock shoes are a must. If the seas are very big you can fish off the bridge at Bare Island or cast a few lures off the nearby Frenchman's Beach.

Try suspending a whole pilchard or garfish under a bobby cork, as the water is fairly deep on the NE side of the point. Use a lightly weighted bait to fish the number of washes that are found here.

Don't forget to take along a few metal slicers for the salmon and tailor that frequent this area. Drummer and luderick are best fish for when using a flat or a small bobby cork. Make sure that you berley well to keep the fish in the area you are fishing.

BAITS AND LURES

Pink nippers, blood worms, peeled Hawkesbury River prawns, mullet and tuna strips. You could also try using strips of chicken breast and bread for bait. Lightly weighted soft plastics like the ZMAN 2.5-inch GrubZ and the 3-inch MinnowZ would be ideal for surface or sub surface.

BEST TIDE/TIMES

This spot can be fished right through the day and night. Make sure that when you are fishing here that you have a small, but steady berley trail going. I would concentrate your fishing time about two to three hours either side of the top of the tide. During the lower parts of the tide I would cast out wide onto the sandy area for bream, trevally, dusky flathead and the odd paned size snapper.

AMENITIES

Toilets, drinking water and a nearby restaurant and kiosk.

KIDS AND FAMILIES

Playground for the kids is nearby. There are a number of nearby walking tracks that will take you out to Henry Head and the Botany Bay National Park. From here you could take a walk along Frenchman's Beach and over to the container wall at Port Botany. If the kids get bored with fishing you could always build sand castles on the beach.

FRENCHMAN'S BAY

🔍 HOW TO GET THERE

When coming in from the west you can travel east along Botany Road. Turn left into Bunnerong Road and then follows this down to the end of Anzac Parade. Parking here can be hard at times and you may have to park in a side street.

Great little sandy beach that is protected in any northerly wind.

🔍 SNAPSHOT

Platform
BEACH & ROCK GROYNES

Target species
BREAM
DUSKY FLATHEAD
SAND WHITING
SILVER TREVALLY
FLOUNDER
AUSTRALIAN SALMON
TAILOR
SQUID.

Best baits
BLOOD WORMS
PINK NIPPERS
WHOLE & HALF PILCHARDS
WHITEBAIT
STRIPS OF MULLET

Best lures
METAL SLICES
SOFT PLASTICS
SOFT VIBES

Best time
EARLY MORNING,
LATE AFTERNOON ON
A FALLING TIDE

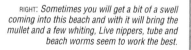

RIGHT: *Sometimes you will get a bit of a swell coming into this beach and with it will bring the mullet and a few whiting, Live nippers, tube and beach worms seem to work the best.*

SEASONS

Bream **February – May**

Dusky flathead
November – April

Flounder
November – April

Salmon **March – June**

Sand whiting
October. – April

Silver trevally
March – June

Tailor **March – August**

This is a small beach that faces south and is best fished in any other wind other than a southerly. Early morning and late afternoons seem to produce the better catches. There is a small breakwall situated a few hundred metres along the beach that is a good spot to cast out from into deeper water..

TACTICS

Great place to take the kids for a fish with their small rods, as they won't have to cast out far. As the bottom is sand, they won't get any snags, unless they hook onto a bit of passing weed or kelp.

Don't forget to take along those plastics and blades that you have as the flathead that feed in close here won't be able to resist them.

I would also take along a couple of rod holders to put in the sand, so that you can leave a bait unattended while you are chucking out a couple of lures.

BAITS AND LURES

Best baits by far for the bream, flathead, flounder and whiting would be blood worms and pink nippers. You could also use pillie tails, strips of mullet and tuna. Chicken breast also goes well here. Great place to work the shoreline with soft plastics and blades, as there are very little snags. Cast out as far as possible and slowly work them back to the shoreline. Small 20 to 40-gram metal work well here for the tailor.

BEST TIDE/TIMES

As the water depth, here is not deep, it is best to fish off the beach at the top of the tide and off the breakwall when the tide is lower.

AMENITIES

Toilets, drinking water and a nearby restaurant and kiosk.

KIDS AND FAMILIES

Playground for the kids is nearby. There are a number of nearby walking tracks that will take you out to Henry Head and the Botany Bay National Park. From here you could take a walk along Frenchman's Beach and over to the container wall at Port Botany. If the kids get bored with fishing you could always build sand castles on the beach.

YARRA BAY SAILING CLUB

HOW TO GET THERE

When coming in from the west you can travel east along Botany Road. Turn left into Bunnerong Road and then follows this down to the end of Anzac Parade. Parking here can be hard at times and you may have to park in a side street. Or you could turn right off Yarra Road and park near the Yarra Bay House.

SNAPSHOT

Platform
BEACH & ROCK
BREAKWALL

Target species
BREAM
DUSKY FLATHEAD
SAND WHITING
SILVER TREVALLY
SQUID

Best baits
BLOOD WORMS
PINK NIPPERS
WHOLE & HALF PILCHARDS
WHITEBAIT
STRIPS OF MULLET

Best lures
METAL SLICERS
SOFT PLASTICS
SOFT VIBES

Best time
EARLY MORNING
LATE AFTERNOON
ON A FALLING TIDE

SEASONS

Bream	**February – May**
Dusky flathead	**November – April**
Sand whiting	**October– April**
Silver trevally	**March – June**
Salmon	**March – June**
Squid	**Year round**
Tailor	**March – August**

ABOVE: *Yarra Bay Sailing Club and breakwall.*

RIGHT: *This point juts out into deep water near the Yarra Bay Sailing Club.*

There is a small breakwall and a rocky point situated east of the sailing club that is worth a shot of bream, flathead, whiting and squid. Salmon and tailor can also be caught from here. Great place to fish in a northerly wind.

TACTICS

This would have to be one of my favourite squid spots at the top of the tide. Once the tide has gone hallway out, I will change over the using soft plastics for flathead and then when the tide is just about all the way out, I will switch to using blades.

BAITS AND LURES

Best baits by far for the bream, flathead, flounder and whiting would be blood worms and pink nippers. You could also use pillie tails, strips of mullet and tuna. Chicken breast also goes well here. Great place to work the shoreline with soft plastics and blades, as there are very little snags. Cast out as far as possible and slowly work them back to the shoreline. Small 20 to 40-gram metal work well here for the tailor.

BEST TIDE/TIMES

Early morning and late afternoon seems to produce the better catches. If it is over cast you can fish right through the day. Night-time fishing from the breakwall can be brilliant at times. You just have to keep an eye out for the water rats, as they can steal your baits.

AMENITIES

Toilets, drinking water and a nearby restaurant and kiosk at the end of Frenchman's Beach.

KIDS AND FAMILIES

Playground for the kids is nearby. There are a number of nearby walking tracks that will take you out to Henry Head and the Botany Bay National Park. From here you could take a walk along Frenchman's Beach and over to the container wall at Port Botany. If the kids get bored with fishing you could always build sand castles on the beach.

COOK RIVER BREAKWALL

🔍 HOW TO GET THERE

If you are travelling from the north, you will need to turn off General Holmes drive just after the turn off to the M5. From here you can drive down into the northern cark park. If you want to go to the southern breakwall you will need to turn off to the left just after you have crossed the Cooks River Bridge. Coming from the south along General Holmes Drive you will need to turn left after you have crossed the Cooks River Bridge. This will take you under the bridge and to the northern carpark.

🔍 SNAPSHOT

Platform
  BEACH & ROCK
  BREAKWALL

Target species
  BREAM
  DUSKY FLATHEAD
  FLOUNDER
  LUDERICK
  SAND WHITING
  SALMON
  SILVER TREVALLY
  SQUID
  TAILOR

Best baits
  BLOOD WORMS
  PINK NIPPERS
  WHOLE & HALF PILCHARDS
  WHITEBAIT
  STRIPS OF MULLET

Best lures
  METAL SLICES
  SOFT PLASTIC
  SOFT VIBES

Best time
  EARLY MORNING,
  LATE AFTERNOON ON
  A FALLING TIDE

SEASONS

Bream **February – May**
Dusky flathead & flounder
November – April
Luderick **Mar. – Sep.**
Sand whitening **Oct. – Apr.**
Salmon **March – June**
Silver trevally **Mar. – Jun.**
Squid **Year round**
Tailor **March to August**

ABOVE: *The southern wall is best fished on a run-out tide for bream, trevally, flathead and luderick.*

LEFT: *Cast out Cranka Crabs and allow them to drift with the current as it moves along the breakwall.*

There is a small breakwall on either side of the entrance to the Cooks River that can be easily accessed. As you sit here having a fish you watch the coming and goings of the planes at the Mascot airport.

TACTICS

If you are after luderick you will need to fish the run-out tide with a stemmed float and make sure that you have a small, but steady stream of berley. Green weed or cabbage mixed up with semi moist sand is the best for berley.

Take two rods so that you can set one rig out wide, while using the other with a lightly weighted bait as you wait for the other to get a bite. To help you land the fish you will need to have a long-handled net. The best position here for bream, trevally and tailor is at the ends of both walls.

BAITS AND LURES

Peeled prawns, strips of tuna and mullet for the bream and trevally. Half pilchards for the dusky flathead and whole pilchards or garfish for the tailor and salmon.

Try suing a variety 3 to 6-inch ZMAN soft plastics on ¼ to 1/6th ounce TT Tournament jig heads for the flathead, salmon and tailor. TT Switchblades would be great for the flathead, as well as bream, whiting and trevally. Make sure you put in a couple of squid jigs.

BEST TIDE/TIMES

This place seems to work much better on the run-out tide. The odd fish or two can be caught on the run-in tide, but I would move to the pontoon that is beside the ramp further upstream.

AMENITIES

The closest amenities to here are the ones that are in the Kyeemagh Reserve at the end of Mutch Avenue Kyeemagh. There are also a few covered picnic tables here as well. To get to here you can go via Mutch Avenue off Bestic Street, Tancred Avenue off General Holmes Drive. There is more parking on the northern side of the river than the southern side.

KIDS AND FAMILIES

On the southern side of the southern wall you will find a sandy beach where the kids can play in the sand or kick a ball around. Just a short walk further south you will come to Cook Park where there is a great playground for the kids. There is a fish and chip shop here that is worth a look at if you don't catch your own.

THE GRAND PARARDE BRIGHTON

HOW TO GET THERE

Either travel east down Bay Street from Rockdale or President Ave from Kogarah until you find The Grand Parade. Then find yourself a parking spot (very popular area) and walk to the beach.

ABOVE: *Whether you are fishing, swimming or sun baking the stretch of shoreline along Brighton has it all.*

LEFT: *An angler waiting for a bite on a rising tide.*

SNAPSHOT

Platform
BEACH & ROCK
GROYNES

Target species
BREAM
DUSKY FLATHEAD
FLOUNDER
SALMON
SAND WHITING
TAILOR

Best baits
BLOOD WORMS
PINK NIPPERS
WHOLE & HALF PILCHARDS
WHITEBAIT
STRIPS OF MULLET

Best lures
METAL SLICES, SOFT PLASTICS,SOFT VIBES

Best time
RISING AND FALLING TIDES

SEASONS

Bream **February to May**

Dusky flathead & flounder **Nov.– Apr.**

Salmon **March– June**

Sand Whiting **October – April**

Tailor **March – August**

During the spring and summer months this is a very popular spot with families as you can have a swim in one of the netted swimming pools found along this stretch of beach. If the fishing isn't that good you could always go across the road to the shops at Brighton-Lee-Sand for a coffee and cake or take the kids for an ice-cream.

It can get crowed here, but this doesn't seem to bother the fish. I would concentrate my fishing times to early morning, late afternoons or into the night.

TACTICS

When fishing here you don't need a long beach rod. A 1.8 to 2.1 metre rod will do the job. I would take two to three rods and some PVC tubes so that you can stick the PVC tubes into the sand. Then cast out your bait and set the drag (not too tight) so that the fish can hook itself. This is where those Owner 1/0 circle hooks come into their own.

Seen that you are allowed to have 4 rods rigged you can also take along a lure outfit and chuck around a few soft plastics and blades for flathead, flounder, bream and whiting that will feed in close along the beach.

BAITS AND LURES

Peeled prawns, strips of tuna and mullet for the bream and trevally. Half pilchards for the dusky flathead and whole pilchards or garfish for the tailor and salmon. Don't forget to also try using pink nippers, blood, tube and beach worms.

Try suing a variety 3 to 6-inch ZMAN soft plastics on 1/4th to 1/6th ounce TT Tournament jig heads for the flathead, salmon and tailor. TT Switchblades would be great for the flathead, as well as bream, whiting and trevally.

BEST TIDE/TIMES

This stretch of beach is best fished a couple of hours either side of the top of the tide. During the lower parts of the tide you will need to cast out much further to get to the feeding fish. During the dark the fish will come in closer to feed.

AMENITIES

Dotted along the foreshore there are a number of toilets. A few of the buildings across the road do have toilets as well. You will also find seating and cover shade dotted along the shoreline as well, and there is a netted swimming pool here as well.

KIDS AND FAMILIES

When the kids tire of fishing you could always kick a ball around on the beach, build sand castles, go for a swim or take them over the road to the shops. There are some great cafes and restaurants at Brighton.

HOW TO GET THERE

Travel east along Ramsgate Road until you reach The Grand Parade. Turn either left or right to find a nearby parking area. When travelling form the north of up from the south you will need to get yourself onto The Grand Parade. Then it's just a matter of finding a parking spot.

SNAPSHOT

Platform
ESTUARY BEACH AND CONCRETE PLATFORM

Target species
BREAM
DUSKY FLATHEAD
FLOUNDER
SAND WHITING
SALMON
TAILOR

Best baits
BLOOD WORMS
PINK NIPPERS
WHOLE & HALF PILCHARDS
WHITEBAIT
STRIPS OF MULLET

Best lures
METAL SLICES , SOFT PLASTICS, SOFT VIBES

Best time
EARLY MORNING, LATE AFTERNOON ON A FALLING TIDE

SEASONS

Bream **February to May**

Dusky flathead & flounder **November to April**

Sand whiting **October to April**

Salmon **March to June**

Tailor **March to August**

ABOVE: *Beach worms and nippers are a great bait for whiting, bream and flathead that can be caught from this stretch of shoreline.*

LEFT: *Not a bad spot to cast out a line or two while resting you rod up against the railing.*

This is a concrete walkway that runs from the Captain Cooks Bridge north to Brighton from where you can fish from. You will need to keep an eye on your casting as a lot of walkers and bike riders traverse along here during the day and night. The baths are very popular during the weekends as they hold nipper's meetings in the baths.

TACTICS

Set yourself up one outfit for using bait and have another outfit where you can cast either soft plastics or blades for bream, flathead, flounder and whiting.

BAITS AND LURES

Best baits by far for the bream, flathead, flounder and whiting would be blood worms and pink nippers. You could also use pillie tails, strips of mullet and tuna. Chicken breast also goes well here.

Great place to work the shoreline with soft plastics and blades, as there are very little snags. Cast out as far as possible and slowly work them back to the shoreline. Small 20 to 40-gram metal work well here for the tailor.

BEST TIDE/TIMES

When fishing from here it doesn't seem to matter whether the tide is rising or falling. As long as it's moving. Night time would be the best. If you don't like the dark, you could always arrive at sun rise or a couple of hours before the sun sets.

AMENITIES

There are nearby toilets and covered seating in the park.

KIDS AND FAMILIES

Great netted swimming pool for when the going gets hot. Nearby playground and grassed area. You will also find a quaint little restaurant called Omeros on the Beach here, as well as a petrol station and a Coles supermarket here.

DOLLS POINT

HOW TO GET THERE

Whether you are travelling north or south along Rocky Point Road you will need to turn down Russell Avenue. Once at the end of the road you will come to a park. Park here and it's a short walk to the beach or walkway that runs from the Capitan Cooks bridge to Brighton.

SNAPSHOT

Platform
BEACH & ROCK
BREAKWALL

Target species
BREAM
DUSKY FLATHEAD
FLOUNDER SAND
WHITING
SALMON
TAILOR

Best baits
BLOOD WORMS
PINK NIPPERS
WHOLE & HALF PILCHARDS
WHITEBAIT
STRIPS OF MULLET

Best lures
METAL SLICERS
SOFT PLASTICS, SOFT
VIBES

Best time
EARLY MORNING, LATE
AFTERNOON ON A
FALLING TIDE

ABOVE: *Looking back from Dolls Point towards Brighton you have a number of groynes that you can fish from.*

LEFT: *This bream fell victim to a lightly weight Gulp 2-inch minnow in camo.*

If you are fishing from the beach care will need to be taken, as there have been a few people swept away from here. When fishing from here don't go into the water as the rushing tide can sweep away the sand before you know it.

TACTICS

Even though there is a public walkway along this stretch of shoreline there are a few places where you can cast a line with either a paternoster rig, a ball sinker down onto the bait or one that has the sinker down onto a swivel with a leader of about a metre in length.

If there is not too much pedestrian traffic you could rest you rod up against the hand rail. Or maybe you could use a strap to vertically fix it to the rail. During the time when there are big seas and there is a bit of swell coming into the bay you should have ago at cast out a few metal slicers or whole pilchards and garfish on a set of gangs for tailor and salmon.

BAITS AND LURES

Half or whole pilchards, garfish, prawns, nipper,

blood and beach worms are the go here. During the cooler months of the year you could try using strips of mullet, tuna, bonito or chicken gut. Don't forget to take along a few 30 to 50-gram metal slicers for the tailor and salmon. Great place to work those soft plastics and blades for flathead.

BEST TIDE/TIMES

A couple of hours either side of the top of the tides works better when fishing from here. As you can use a shorter rod, because you don't have to cast as far. Early morning or late afternoon or even during the night is ideal for here. When it's raining, you don't seem to get as much pedestrian traffic here during the day.

AMENITIES

Several toilets are in the park.

KIDS AND FAMILIES

There is a large park situated here and there are a number of covered picnic tables and shelters. Great place for a picnic, while you go for a fish. Plenty of room to kick or throw a ball around.

SEASONS

Bream
February to May

Dusky flathead & flounder **Nov.– Apr.**

Sand whiting
October to April

Salmon **March to June**

Tailor **March to August**

GEORGE'S RIVER 16FT SAILING CLUB

🔍 HOW TO GET THERE

Whether you are travelling north or south along Rocky Point Road you will need to turn down Russell Avenue. Once at the end of the road you will come to a park. Park here and it's a short walk to the beach or walkway that runs from the Capitan Cooks bridge to Brighton.

🔍 SNAPSHOT

Platform
SANDY BEACH
WEEDY PATCHES
DEEP TIDAL FLOW

Target species
BREAM
DUSKY FLATHEAD
FLOUNDER
SAND WHITING

Best baits
BLOOD WORMS
PINK NIPPERS
WHOLE & HALF PILCHARDS
WHITEBAIT
STRIPS OF MULLET

Best lures
METAL SLICES,
SURFACE POPPERS,
SOFT VIBES, SURFACE
POPPERS

Best time
EARLY MORNING,
LATE AFTERNOON ON
A FALLING TIDE

SEASONS

Bream
February to May

Dusky flathead & flounder
November to April

Sand whiting
October to April

ABOVE: *The stretch of sand north of the club is very popular for bream, whiting and flathead.*

LEFT: *Yabbies can be pumped here at low tide and then used to catch whiting and bream.*

This spot is best fishing at low tide during the day and high tide at night. Great place to take the family for a fish. There is a small nipper ground adjacent to the sailing club.

TACTICS

Make sure that if you are fishing at low tide that you keep an eye on the water as it can rise around the back of you. Maybe take two rods and set one up in a PVC rod holder for whiting and bream, while you work those lures for the flathead and bream that can be caught here. The odd flounder can be caught here during the warmer months.

BAITS AND LURES

At low tide, you could try pumping a few pink nippers here that you could then use as bait. If not, I would try either blood or beach worms for whiting, bream and flathead. Great place to have ago with soft plastics and blades as you can cast out wide into deep water. Remember to work them back to where you are standing in small, but slow hops.

BEST TIDE/TIMES

A couple of hours either side of the top of the tides works better when fishing from here. As you can use a shorter rod, because you don't have to cast as far. Early morning or late afternoon or even during the night is ideal for here. When it's raining, you don't seem to get as much pedestrian traffic here during the day.

AMENITIES

Several toilets are in the nearby park

KIDS AND FAMILIES

There is a large park situated here and there are a number of covered picnic tables and shelters. Great place for a picnic, while you go for a fish. Plenty of room to kick or throw a ball around.

BONNAPOINT/SILVER BEACH

HOW TO GET THERE

The spot is located on the southern side of Botany Bay at Kurnell. To get there you will need to travel along Captain Cook drive. Once you reach the round-a-bout near the shops at Kurnell you will need to turn left into Torries Street. Follow this street until you reach the T section at Charles Parade.

ABOVE: *Along Silver beach you will find a number of groynes that are worth fishing from.*

SNAPSHOT

Platform
  SANDY BEACH &
  ROCK BREAKWALL

Target species
  BREAM
  DUSKY FLATHEAD
  FLOUNDER
  SAND WHITING
  TAILOR

Best baits
  BLOOD WORMS
  PINK NIPPERS
  WHOLE & HALF PILCHARDS
  WHITEBAIT
  STRIPS OF MULLET

Best lures
  METAL SLICERS,
  SOFT PLASTICS,
  SOFT VIBES

Best time
  EARLY MORNING,
  LATE AFTERNOON
  ON A FALLING TIDE

SEASONS

Bream
February to May

Dusky flathead & flounder
November to April

Sand whiting
October to April

Tailor
March to August

LEFT: *This stretch of shoreline is best fished about an hour either side of the top of the tide.*

There is a small, but very productive sandy point at the end of the point that drops off into about four to five metres of water. When you arrive there, you will see a couple of yellow markers on your left-hand side. You cannot fish on the left of them as it is completely closed to all types of fishing.

TACTICS

There are a number of groynes sticking out at ninety degrees to the shoreline. If you are going to walk out on them, you will need to have a good pair of shoes and care will need to be taken as many of the rocks do move around. You can try lure fishing from here for dusky flathead, whiting and bream a couple of hours either side of the top of the tide.

BAITS AND LURES

Half or whole pilchards, garfish, prawns, nipper, blood and beach worms are the go here. During the cooler months of the year you could try using strips of mullet, tuna, bonito or chicken gut. Don't forget to take along a few 30 to 50-gram metal slicers for the tailor and salmon. Great place to work those soft plastics and blades for flathead.

BEST TIDE/TIMES

If you are going to fish off the beach along this stretch of shoreline it would be best to do this a couple of hours either side of the top of the tide. As the tide gets much lower you might think about carefully walking out along one of the many groynes that are also found here.

AMENITIES

There are toilets at Bonna Point and in the Botany Bay National Park. Parking, playground and dog of leash area.

KIDS AND FAMILIES

The water here looks very inviting here for a swim. But at the time of writing there had been a dog taken by a shark at Bonna Point. The owner was throwing a stick out into the water and the dog was chasing it. If you are going to go for a swim you should go in the netted tidal pool found here.

On the weekends the local sailing club will hold races here and it is also a popular place for wind surfing or sail boarding during high winds. About halfway along Charles Parade you will find a small shop that serves hot and cold foods. It is also the local post office.

SUTHERLAND POINT-BOTANY BAY NATIONAL PARK

🔍 HOW TO GET THERE

The spot is located on the southern side of Botany Bay at Kurnell. To get there you will need to travel along Captain Cook drive. Once you reach the round-a-bout near the shops at Kurnell you will via off to the right. Once you reach the T section you will need to turn left and this will lead you to Charles Parade. Then it's just a short 10-minute walk to Sutherland Point through the Botany Bay National Park.

🔍 SNAPSHOT

Platform
ROCK PLATFORM
OCEAN SWELL

Target species
BREAM
DRUMMER
DUSKY FLATHEAD
FLOUNDER, GROPER
SAND WHITING
SALMON, TAILOR
SILVER TREVALLY

Best baits
BLOOD WORMS
PINK NIPPERS
WHOLE & HALF PILCHARDS
WHITEBAIT
STRIPS OF MULLET

Best lures
METAL SLICES
SOFT PLASTICS, SOFT
VIBES

Best time
LOW SWELL, EARLY
MORNING, LATE
AFTERNOON ON A
FALLING TIDE

SEASONS

Bream **February to May**
Drummer **Mar. – Aug.**
Dusky flathead & flounder
Nov. – Apr.
Groper **Year round**
Sand whiting **Oct. – Apr.**
Salmon **March to June**
Silver Trevally **Year round**
Tailor **March to August**

ABOVE: *Sutherland Point is best fished on a rising tide early in the morning for bream, trevally, squid and drummer.*

LEFT: *Try using lightly weighted red crabs for groper here at the top of the tide.*

This is classified as a rock platform and you will need to take care when fishing from here. The swell can get very big here, so much so the point is a very famous surfing spot.

Just about anything can be caught while fishing from here. If the swell is up, I would suggest that you fish inside the point where the white-water ends. Part of Sutherland Point is an IPAs and the collecting of seashore animals is strictly prohibited in these closures. This includes crabs, snails, cunjevoi, octopus, sea urchins, anemones, pipis, cockles, mussels, oysters, and nippers. The area extends from the mean high-water mark to 10 metres seaward from the mean low water mark. Fishing is permitted in these areas, but bait collection is not allowed, although you may bring bait with you up to the quantity allowed by NSW Fisheries.

TACTICS

Predominately this is a rock fishing point and can be fished in most seas. There are a few small pockets of sandy beaches dotted along this point. In the shallower areas, I would try fishing with a half pilchard or peeled prawn underneath a bobby cork. You could also try using a very small ball sinker down onto the top of the bait. Make sure that you stay in contact with the bait at all times to avoid snags.

BAITS AND LURES

Peeled prawns, half pillies, strips of mullet and tuna. You could also try using cunje and bread for bait. Remember to burley. Cast out into the deeper water with 40 to 60-gram metal slicers for tailor and salmon. Don't forget to take along a few squid jigs for the big squid that feed here during the cooler months of the year.

BEST TIDE/TIMES

A couple of hours either side of the top of the tide is the best time to fish. If you would prefer to fish during the lower tides, I would suggest that you use a rod of between 1o to 12 feet in length and the rig should be a double hook paternoster.

AMENITIES

The Botany Bay National Park has a kiosk, toilets, museum, picnic tables, covered areas and fresh running water. Remember if you park your car inside here there is a parking fee that needs to be paid at the office.

KIDS AND FAMILIES

There are a couple of playgrounds, plenty of bush walking tracks and plenty of room to kick a ball around. No dogs are allowed in here. Great place for a picnic.

CAPTAIN COOK BRIDGE

HOW TO GET THERE

Travelling south from Ramsgate along Rocky Point Road you will need to veer off to the right into the carpark, just before you go over the bridge. Travelling north from Caringbah along Taren Point Road you will need to turn left at the last set of lights at Holt Road. Continue down to the small parking area at the foot of the bridge.

SNAPSHOT

Platform
ROCK BREAKWALL

Target species
BREAM
DUSKY FLATHEAD
LUDERICK
MULLET
MULLOWAY
SAND WHITING
SALMON
SILVER TREVALLY
TAILOR

Best baits
BLOOD WORMS
PINK NIPPERS
WHOLE & HALF PILCHARDS
WHITEBAIT
STRIPS OF MULLET
GREEN WEED
PUDDING BAITS

Best lures
METAL SLICES, SOFT PLASTICS, SOFT VIBES

Best time
RISING AND FALLING TIDES

SEASONS
Bream **Feb. – May**
Dusky flathead **Nov.– Apr.**
Luderick **Mar.– Sep.**
Mullet **Yera round**
Mulloway **Year round**
Sand whiting **Oct.– Apr.**
Salmon **Mar.–Jun**
Silver trevally **Jan. – May**
Tailor **Mar.– Aug.**

ABOVE: *The ramp at the southern side of the Captain Cook Bridge can be slippery at low tide. Be careful.*

RIGHT: *Ideal spot to fish the run-out tide on the southern side of the bridge.*

Both the northern and southern side of the bridge will produce fish during the day or night. The main thing that I would worry about at night is the big bait and fish stealing rats that live here. On the southern side, there is the old ferry ramp that can be fished from, but you will need to take care as it can be extremely slippery.

TACTICS
Work those larger weighted jig heads and plastics out wide for dusky flathead and mulloway during the slower parts of the tide. Top or bottom of the tide doesn't seem to matter. You could also suspend a whole pilchards or garfish under a bobby cork for tailor and salmon.

BAITS AND LURES
Peeled prawns, nippers and blood worms would be the go here for bream, trevally and sand whiting. Don't forget to have a few metal slicers for those tailor that are just out of reach when using baits.

BEST TIDE/TIMES
Both the run-in and run-out tides will produce fish here. If you are after a few mullet and luderick the run-out tide on the southern side is the best and the run-in on the northern side.

AMENITIES
On the southern side of the bridge there are no amenities. On the northern side, there are a set of toilets and the Sand Souci swimming pool. These are on the outside of the pool building.

KIDS AND FAMILIES
Not much to do for the kids on the southern side of the bridge unless they want to fish or watch the boats go by. The northern side has a park, covered picnic tables, a playground, a floating pontoon and a swimming pool. There are also a couple of nearby cafes and restaurants.

THE PROMONARDE-KOGARAH BAY

🔍 HOW TO GET THERE

Whether you are travelling north from Blakehurst or South from Kogarah along the Princes Highway you will need to turn into Park Road which then turns into Ramsgate Road. As you are travelling east you will find the Beverley Park Golf Course on your left and Claydon Reserve on your right. Parking can be found in nearby side streets.

🔍 SNAPSHOT

Platform
ROCK BREAKWALL

Target species
BREAM,
DUSKY FLATHEAD,
MULLET
SAND WHITENING

Best baits
BLOOD WORMS
PINK NIPPERS
HALF PILCHARDS
WHITEBAIT
STRIPS OF MULLET
PUDDING BAITS

Best lures
METAL SLICES
SOFT PLASTICS
SOFT VIBES

Best time
EITHER SIDE OF THE
HIGH TIDE

SEASONS

Bream
February– May

Dusky flathead
November to April

Mulloway
Year round

Sand whiting
October to April

ABOVE: *Either fish from the deck at low tide or the rock wall during the higher tides.*

RIGHT: *Best fished either side of the top of the tide, as it is very shallow here.*

You will find a soccer field on the opposite side of the road to the Beverley Hill golf course where you can fish in about a metre and a half of water at the top of the tide for bream, flathead, whiting and mullet. On the western side of the bay is a concrete storm water culvert that runs through the gold course and out into the bay. Poddy mullet can be caught here. New casting platform here as well.

TACTICS

Due to the water depth being not that deep here towards the bottom of the tide you will mainly need to concentrate your fishing time to near the top of the tide. Try putting in a poddy mullet trap and getting a few live mullet for the bigger dusky flathead that can be caught here. If you are after mullet, I would use a small bobby cork and suspend some bread or fish pudding underneath. Make sure that you berley to keep the fish in the area.

BAITS AND LURES

Strips of mullet. Half pilchards and tuna would be the go here. You could also try pink nippers and blood worms for the bream and whiting. Bread would be great for the mullet. Make sure that you take a few soft plastics with you.

BEST TIDE/TIMES

High tide is best by far the best time to fish here as the fish will come in closer to the shore. Try fishing here at night when there is a high tide.

AMENITIES

There are toilets near the small boat ramp in the eastern corner of the bay.

KIDS AND FAMILIES

The weekend during the cooler months of the years it can get very crowed here due to a lot of local sport going on. Better fished during the week or late into the afternoon.

CARSS PARK BATHS

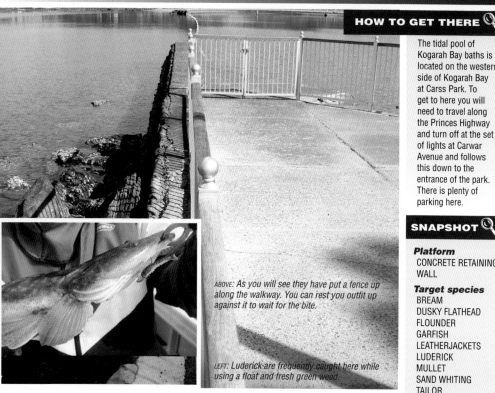

HOW TO GET THERE

The tidal pool of Kogarah Bay baths is located on the western side of Kogarah Bay at Carss Park. To get to here you will need to travel along the Princes Highway and turn off at the set of lights at Carwar Avenue and follows this down to the entrance of the park. There is plenty of parking here.

ABOVE: As you will see they have put a fence up along the walkway. You can rest you outfit up against it to wait for the bite.

LEFT: Luderick are frequently caught here while using a float and fresh green weed.

SNAPSHOT

Platform
CONCRETE RETAINING WALL

Target species
BREAM
DUSKY FLATHEAD
FLOUNDER
GARFISH
LEATHERJACKETS
LUDERICK
MULLET
SAND WHITING
TAILOR

Best baits
BLOOD WORMS
PINK NIPPERS
WHOLE & HALF PILCHARDS
WHITEBAIT
STRIPS OF MULLET
GREEN WEED
PUDDING BAITS

Best lures
METAL SLICERS, SOFT PLASTICS, SOFT VIBES

Best time
RISING AND FALLING TIDES

SEASONS
Bream **Feb.– May**
Dusky flathead
Nov.– Apr.
Garfish **Year round**
Flounder **Nov.– Apr.**
Latherjackets **Year round**
Luderick **Mar.– Sep.**
Sand whiting **Oct.– April**
salmon **Mar.– June**
Tailor **Mar.– Aug.**

C arss Bush Park is located on the foreshore of Kogarah Bay, off Carwar Avenue, Carss Park. The park land consists of a relatively large area of public open space. The area now known as Carss Bush Park was originally part of Jonathon Croft's 54 hectares of land that was purchased from the Crown in 1854.

TACTICS
Due to the water depth being not that deep here towards the bottom of the tide you will mainly need to concentrate your fishing time to near the top of the tide. Try putting in a poddy mullet trap and getting a few live mullet for the bigger dusky flathead that can be caught here. If you are after mullet I would use a small bobby cork and suspend some bread or fish pudding underneath. Make sure that you berley to keep the fish in the area.

BAITS AND LURES
Whole pilchards and garfish for the tailor. Pillie tails, blood worms, nippers and chicken pieces for the bream and leatherjackets. Green weed for the luderick and bread for the mullet.

BEST TIDE/TIMES
At either side of the tidal pool there is a small walkway on top of the sandstone retaining wall. You can fish from here for mullet, luderick, leatherjackets and the odd garfish or two.

Cast out wide when the tide is low for bream, flathead and the odd flounder or two. The odd larger tailor can be caught off here when casting out metal slicers or suspending a whole pilchard or garfish under a float.

AMENITIES
Carss Bush Park offers a wide variety of recreational facilities and services. These include the Carss Park Café and Grill, the Kogarah War Memorial Olympic Swimming Pool, sports fields, bushland, playground areas, picnic and BBQ facilities, an intertidal swimming area, a Life Savers building, internal car parks, a stage area and other amenities and infrastructure

KIDS AND FAMILIES
If the kids get sick of fishing and they want something else to do, they can play and ride in the large playground that is here. During the warmer months, they can go for a swim in the tidal pool or just play on the beach.

TOM UGLY'S BRIDGE

🔍 HOW TO GET THERE

Travelling south from Blakehurst along the Princes Highway to will need look out for the turn off to the left that will take you down to a parking area on the north side of the bridge. Travelling north from Sylvania and the Prince Highway you will need to turn off to the right just before the bridge and go down to the parking area situated under the bridge.

🔍 SNAPSHOT

Platform
ROCKWALL
CONCRETE PLATFORM
BOAT RAMP WITH
PONTOON

Target species
BREAM
DUSKY FLATHEAD
FLOUNDER
LEATHERJACKETS
LUDERICK, MULLERT
SAND WHITING
SILVER TREVALLY
TAILOR, SQUID

Best baits
BLOOD WORMS
PINK NIPPERS
WHOLE & HALF PILCHARDS
WHITEBAIT
STRIPS OF MULLET
GREEN WEED
PUDDING BAITS

Best lures
METAL SLICERS, SOFT PLASTICS, SOFT VIBES

Best time
RISING AND FALLING TIDES

SEASONS

Bream **Feb.– May**
Dusky flathead **Nov.– April**
Flounder **Nov.– Apr.**
Leatherjacket **Year round**
Luderick **Mar. – Sep.**
Mullet **Year round**
Sand whitening **Oct.– Apr.**
Silver trevally **Mar.– Jun.**
Tailor **Mar.– Aug.**
Squid **Year round**

ABOVE: *This boat ramp is used a lot by commercial outfits, but can be fished when they are either loading or unloading their gear. Great spot at night.*

RIGHT: *Try flicking out either soft plastics, metals or whole pilchards off the pontoon here in the early hours of the morning on a rising tide.*

Both the northern and southern side of the bridge will produce fish during the day or night. The main thing that I would worry about at night is the big bait and fish stealing rats that live here. On the southern side, there is the old ferry ramp that is now a boat ramp that can be fished from, but you will need to take care as it can be extremely slippery. There is also a wharf that extends out towards the bridge pylon.

TACTICS

The best rig to use here would be the paternoster, as the bottom is very snaggy under the bridge and on the upstream side. A running ball sinker down onto the swivel and a long leader would be ok on the downstream side.

BAITS AND LURES

Pink nippers, blood worms, pilchards and strips of squid, mullet and tuna would be the go here. All these baits can be purchased from Macs Bait Bar on the northern side of the bridge.

BEST TIDE/TIMES

Fishing here can be carried out during the run-in and run-out tides. You will just need to position yourself so that your lines don't run across the boat ramp.

AMENITIES

On the eastern side of the bridge there is a small marina where you can get a drink or maybe a coffee.

KIDS AND FAMILIES

Small playground nearby.

ABOVE: *This large squid fell to a well-presented Fish Inc squid jig.*

HOW TO GET THERE

Whether you are travelling south from Blakehurst or north from Sylvania along the Prince Highway you will need to turn off at Stuart Street. Follow this down to the end and then park your car. From here it is a short walk down along a track that leads to the water.

SNAPSHOT

Platform
ROCK POINT WITH DEEP WATER

Target species
BREAM
DUSKY FLATHEAD
FLOUNDER
LEATHERJACKETS
MULLET
MULLOWAY
SAND WHITING
SILVER TREVALLY
LUDERICK

Best baits
BLOOD WORMS
PINK NIPPERS
WHOLE & HALF PILCHARDS
WHITEBAIT
STRIPS OF MULLET
GREEN WEED
PUDDING BAITS

Best lures
METAL SLICERS, SOFT PLASTICS, SOFT VIBES

Best time
RISING AND FALLING TIDES

SEASONS

Bream **Feb.– May**
Dusky flathead **Nov.– Apr.**
Flounder **Nov.– Apr.**
Leatherjacket **Year round**
Luderick **Mar.– Sep**
Mullet **Year round**
Mulloway **Oct.– May**
Sand whiting **Oct.– Apr.**
Silver trevally **Mar.– Jun.**

This is a great spot to have a fish when the conditions are coming from the north. Most of the southern and western side of this point has deep water and is best fished on a rising tide. The northern side is best fished on an out-going tide and a descent cast will get you out onto a sandy bottom. The tide can race around here at times.

TACTICS

Longer rods between 3 to 3.6 metres in length would be the preferred length. Both the paternoster rig and the running ball sinker down onto the swivel with a longer leader can be used here. When the tide slackens, you could try changing to the small running ball sinker down onto the bait. Remember to take a few 30 to 60-gram metal slicers for the tailor that frequent here.

BAITS AND LURES

Squid, pilchards, garfish, strips of tuna and mullet, pink nippers, blood worms and strips of chicken breast are the go here.

BEST TIDE/TIMES

When the tide is coming in it's better to fish on the upstream side of the point as your baits will go out away from the snaggy bottom that is in close. You could try suspending a whole squid. Pilchard or garfish underneath a bobby cork.

Don't forget to take a few soft plastics with you. Bunny hop them off the bottom for dusky flathead and mulloway. There are a few big ones to be found here

AMENITIES

No toilets here.

KIDS AND FAMILIES

Not a lot to do here for the kids. Except to fish and go exploring along the shoreline.

OATLEY BAY BOAT RAMP

HOW TO GET THERE

Whether travelling south from Penshurst or north from South Hurstville along King Georges Road you will need to turn off at Hillcrest Avenue. Then turn left at Lansdowne Street and then into Watara Parade. It's then a short distance to The Crescent, West Crescent and then Moreshead Drive.

SNAPSHOT

Platform
ESTUARY ROCKS
DEEP WATER

Target species
BREAM
DUSKY FLATHEAD
FLOUNDER
SAND WHITING
MULLET
LUDERICK

Best baits
BLOOD WORMS
PINK NIPPERS
WHOLE & HALF PILCHARDS
WHITEBAIT
STRIPS OF MULLET
PUDDING BAITS

Best lures
METAL SLICERS, SOFT
PLASTICS, SOFT VIBES

Best time
RISING AND FALLING
TIDES

SEASONS

Bream **Feb.– May**

Dusky flathead &
flounder **Nov.– Apr.**

Sand whiting **Oct.– Apr.**

Garfish, leatherjacket,
Mullet **Year round**

Luderick **Mar.– Sep.**

ABOVE: Heavily used boat ramp at times. Care needs to be taken when fishing from here. Try the shoreline on either side of the ramp.

As this is a boat ramp it can get very busy at times, so you will need to give way to the boaters. You can fish on either side of the boat ramp. On the right-hand side, there is a small beach and on the left-hand side there is a few mangroves and rocks. A wooden lookout on the edge of Moore Reserve offers a beautiful view through the swamp trees. With tree-covered peninsulas on either side of the bay, it really feels like a retreat down here. In late spring, flowering Jacaranda trees add more colour to the scene.

TACTICS

You don't need a long rod when fishing from here. Try using a small ball sinker down onto the bait or a running ball sinker down onto a swivel with a long leader. Soft plastics and hard bodied lures would be ideal for here as there a very little in the way of snags.

Maybe you could work the front of the mangroves on the left-hand side of the ramp.

BAITS AND LURES

Squid, pilchards, garfish, strips of tuna and mullet, pink nippers, blood worms and strips of chicken breast are the go here.

BEST TIDE/TIMES

Early morning and late afternoons when the tide is a couple of hours either side of the top would be best here as you don't have to cast as far. If you go, there when the tide is low you could fish on the sandy area on the right-hand side of the ramp. Try using soft plastic like the ZMan Slim SwimmerZ and grubs for bream whiting and flathead.

AMENITIES

BBQ, picnic, toilets, playground, parking, boat ramp, cycleway, walking track and off the lease dog area.

KIDS AND FAMILIES

Moore Reserve is a great green hideaway from the busy world. It has a sprawling grassy field complete with recreational facilities. Enjoy picnics and barbecues, a cycleway and walking track, and play equipment for the kids.

OATLEY POINT

HOW TO GET THERE

Whether travelling south from Penshurst or north from South Hurstville along King Georges Road you will need to turn off at Hillcrest Avenue. Then turn left at Rosa Street. It's a short distance down to Algernon or Herbert Street on the right. Oatley Point Park is at the end of the road.

ABOVE: *Snapper at times will frequent this deep-water spot, along with bream, flathead and tailor.*

SNAPSHOT

Platform
CONCRETE RETAINING WALL

Target species
BREAM
DUSKY FLATHEAD
FLOUNDER
MULLET
MULLOWAY
SAND WHITING

Best baits
BLOOD WORMS
PINK NIPPER
WHOLE & HALF PILCHARDS
WHITEBAIT
STRIPS OF MULLET
GREEN WEED
PUDDING BAITS

Best lures
METAL SLICERS
SOFT PLASTICS
SOFT VIBES

Best time
RISING AND
FALLING TIDES

Fishing from this point can be extremely productive at times and is one of my favourite flathead and bream spots. As you will be fishing from the rocks here you will need to make sure that you have non-slippery footwear. Also, as this is the point at the entrance to Oatley Bay a long cast is need to get you out into the channel, but you will need to watch out for passing boats.

TACTICS
Longer rods between 3 to 3.6 metres in length would be the preferred length. Both the paternoster rig and the running ball sinker down onto the swivel with a longer leader can be used here. When the tide slackens, you could try changing to the small running ball sinker down onto the bait. Remember to take a few 30 to 60-gram metal slicers for the tailor that frequent here.

BAITS AND LURES
Squid, pilchards, garfish, strips of tuna and mullet, pink nippers, blood worms and strips of chicken breast are the go here.

BEST TIDE/TIMES
When the tide is coming in it's better to fish on the upstream side of the point as your baits will go out away from the snaggy bottom that is in close. You could try suspending a whole squid. Pilchard or garfish underneath a bobby cork.

Don't forget to take a few soft plastics with you. Bunny hop them off the bottom for dusky flathead and mulloway. There are a few big ones to be found here

AMENITIES
Parking and walking tracks only. No Toilets.

KIDS AND FAMILIES
The kids could go bush walking or explore the bush land in Oatley Park Reserve if they get bored from fishing. Care will need to be taken when fishing from the rocks here as they can be slippery at times.

SEASONS

Bream **Feb.– May**

Dusky flathead &
flounder **Nov.– Apr.**

Mullet **Year round**

Mulloway **Year round**

Sand whiting **Oct.– Apr.**

ABOVE: *This gentleman was targeting mullet to use later as bait.*

HOW TO GET THERE

Find your way to Jannali Railway Station and then head north along Railway Crescent, into Novara Crescent and then into Cremona Road. At the end of the road you will find parking near the Como bridge. There are a couple of cafes and a marina here that you could get yourself a coffee and cake or a milkshake.

SNAPSHOT

Platform
STEP ROCK BREAKWALL

Target species
BREAM
DUSKY FLATHEAD
FLOUNDER
LEATHERJACKETS
LUDERICK
MULLET
MULLOWAY
SAND WHITING
TAILOR

Best baits
BLOOD WORMS
PINK NIPPER
WHOLE & HALF PILCHARDS
WHITEBAIT
STRIPS OF MULLET

Best lures
LARGE SOFT PLASTICS
SOFT VIBES, METAL SLICERS

Best time
RISING AND FALLING TIDES

SEASONS

Bream **Feb.– May**

Dusky flathead **Nov.– Apr.**

Flounder **Nov.– Apr.**

Leatherjacket **Year round**

Luderick **Mar.– Sep.**

Mullet **Year round**

Mulloway **Spring to Autumn**

Sand whiting **Oct.– Apr.**

Tailor **Dec.– Apr**

Great place to bring the family to have a picnic, while at the same you can cast a line into deep water for a flathead, bream or whiting. This spot is also close to the base of the Como Bridge. So, if the fish are not biting here it is just a matter of move to another fishing spot.

The northern side of the bridge is not the easiest land-based spot to get to, but when you do it can be extremely fishy. Big mulloway, dusky flathead and bream can be caught from here. The current does run through here fairly quickly during the middle of the tide and it can be very snaggy at times. The southern side is easier to get to via a walkway/bike track.

TACTICS

Cast out wide with either a paternoster rig or a running ball sinker down onto the bait. Fish from the downstream wharf and retaining wall on the run-out tide and when the tide starts to run-in change to the wharf on the upstream side of the river.

Try using soft plastics and blades for bream and flathead off here. Don't forget to take a few 30 to 50-gram metal slicers with you for the tailor that occasionally feed here

BAITS AND LURES

Squid, pilchards, garfish, strips of tuna and mullet, pink nippers, blood worms and strips of chicken breast are the go here.

BEST TIDE/TIMES

When the tide is coming in it's better to fish on the upstream side of the point as your baits will go out away from the snaggy bottom that is in close. You could try suspending a whole squid. Pilchard or garfish underneath a bobby cork.

Don't forget to take a few soft plastics with you. Bunny hop them off the bottom for dusky flathead and mulloway. There are a few big ones to be found here

AMENITIES

Como Pleasure Grounds is a popular park that contains a playground, toilets, picnic tables and BBQs as well as a bike track and walking loop path.

KIDS AND FAMILIES

There are panoramic views of the Georges River and surrounding bushland from the top of the knoll. You can fish from either end of the tidal netted swimming pool or off the sandstone breakwall. There is also a nearby boat ramp and wharf that you can also cast a bait or lure from.

You will need to get to King Georges Road at Penshurst and then travel down Forest Road. Once you have reached boundary Road you will then need to go to Gungah Bay Road and then turn left into Douglas Haig Street. Oatley Park where the baths are situated can be found on the loop road in the park.

ABOVE: *As you will see there has to be some repair done to the concrete area. Best fished an hour either side of the top of the tide.*

Oatley Park is popular with visitors all year round enjoying a variety of recreational and sporting activities from picnics in Steamroller Park, swimming in the Baths in Sandy Bay to enjoying the many walking tracks and cycleways.

TACTICS

Due to the water depth being not that deep here towards the bottom of the tide you will mainly need to concentrate your fishing time to near the top of the tide. Try putting in a poddy mullet trap and getting a few live mullet for the bigger dusky flathead that can be caught here. If you are after mullet I would use a small bobby cork and suspend some bread or fish pudding underneath. Make sure that you berley to keep the fish in the area.

BAITS AND LURES

Whole pilchards and garfish for the tailor. Pillie tails, blood worms, nippers and chicken pieces for the bream and leatherjackets. Green weed for the luderick and bread for the mullet.

BEST TIDE/TIMES

At either side of the tidal pool there is a small walkway on top of the sandstone retaining wall. You can fish from here for mullet, luderick, leatherjackets and the odd garfish or two. Cast out wide when the tide is low for bream, flathead and the odd flounder or two. The odd larger tailor can be caught off here when casting out metal slicers or suspending a whole pilchard or garfish under a float.

AMENITIES

You will find toilet, covered picnic tables, walking tracks, playground areas, BBQ's and a tidal netted swimming pool.

KIDS AND FAMILIES

The 45-hectare Oatley Park is on a promontory jutting into George's River, bounded by Lime Kiln Bay and Jewfish Bay. Noted for its trees, shrubs and native flowers, as well as the river beaches and prolific bird life. The records do not show when the baths were built but they are known to have been in use in 1919.

The gates are opened approximately at 6:30am all year round and are closed at 6:00pm June, July & August, 7:00pm April, May, September & October and 8:00pm November through to March.

SNAPSHOT 🔍

Platform
CONCRETE RETAINING WALL

Target species
BREAM
DUSKY FLATHEAD
FLOUNDER
MULLOWAY
SAND WHITING

Best baits
BLOOD WORMS
PINK NIPPER
WHOLE & HALF PILCHARDS
WHITEBAIT
STRIPS OF MULLET
GREEN WEED
PUDDING BAITS

Best lures
METAL SLICERS
SOFT PLASTICS
SOFT VIBES

Best time
RISING AND
FALLING TIDES

SEASONS

Bream **Feb.– May**
Dusky flathead
Nov.– April
Flounder
Nov.– April
Mulloway
Spring to Autumn
Sand whiting
Oct.– April

LUGARNO WALKWAY

🔍 HOW TO GET THERE

To get to this spot you will need to get onto Forest Road and travel south until you reach the end of the road where the old Lugarno ferry was.

🔍 SNAPSHOT

Platform
TIMBER WALKWAY
OLD FERRY RAMP

Target species
BREAM
DUSKY FLATHEAD
FLOUNDER
LEATHERJACKETS
LUDERICK
MULLOWAY
SAND WHITING
TAILOR

Best baits
BLOOD WORMS
PINK NIPPERS
WHOLE & HALF PILCHARDS
WHITEBAIT
STRIPS OF MULLET
GREEN WEED
PUDDING BAITS

Best lure
METAL SLICERS, SOFT PLASTICS, SOFT VIBES

Best time
RISING AND FALLING TIDES

SEASONS

Bream   **Feb.– May**

Dusky flathead
Nov.– Apr.

Flounder **Nov.– Apr.**

Leatherjackets
Year round

Luderick
During the cooler months.

Mulloway **Spring to Autumn**

Sand whiting **Oct.– Apr.**

Tailor **Mar– Aug.**

ABOVE: *This angler had a number of rods set to try for a bream or mulloway on the rising tide.*

RIGHT: *Mulloway can be caught off this walkway. Try using ¼ to 1/2oz blades cast out wide and bounce them along with the current.*

Parking can be a bitch here both day and night, but if you go here during the week you should be okay. There is a timbered walkway that you can fish from into deep water. Can get a bit snaggy at times. This spot looks directly over to spot 24; The Old Ferry Road at Illawong and there is a nearby seafood restaurant.

TACTICS

Set yourself up one outfit for using bait and have another outfit where you can cast either soft plastics or blades for bream, flathead, flounder and whiting.

BAITS AND LURES

Best baits by far for the bream, flathead, flounder and whiting would be blood worms and pink nippers. You could also use pillie tails, strips of mullet and tuna. Chicken breast also goes well here. Great place to work the shoreline with soft plastics and blades, as there are very little snags. Cast out as far as possible and slowly work them back to the shoreline. Small 20 to 40-gram metal work well here for the tailor.

BEST TIDE/TIMES

When fishing from here it doesn't seem to matter whether the tide is rising or falling. As long as it's moving. Night time would be the best. If you don't like the dark, you could always arrive at sun rise or a couple of hours before the sun sets.

AMENITIES

No toilets or any other amenities are found here. You will need to travel back up Forest Road to find any.

KIDS AND FAMILIES

At low tide the kids might want to explore the rocks near the ramp. Remember it can be very slippery.

OLD FERRY ROAD ILLAWONG

HOW TO GET THERE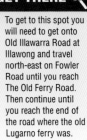

To get to this spot you will need to get onto Old Illawarra Road at Illawong and travel north-east on Fowler Road until you reach The Old Ferry Road. Then continue until you reach the end of the road where the old Lugarno ferry was.

SNAPSHOT

Platform
CONCRETE RETAINING WALL

Target species
BREAM
DUSKY FLATHEAD
SAND WHITING
LUDERICK

Best baits
BLOOD WORMS
PINK NIPPERS
WHOLE & HALF PILCHARDS
WHITEBAIT
STRIPS OF MULLET
PUDDING BAITS

Best lures
SMALL AND LARGE SOFT PLASTICS
SOFT AND METAL VIBES

Best time
RISING AND FALLING TIDES

SEASONS

Bream **Feb.– May**

Dusky flathead
Nov.– Apr.

Sand whiting **Oct.– Apr.**

Luderick **Mar.– Sep.**

ABOVE: *This stretch of water is quite deep and the odd jewfish has been caught here, along with bream, whiting and flathead. NOTE: Change existing picture to the new one supplied.*

LEFT: *When the water clears up the silver trevally will venture up to the Lugarno stretch of the river.*

This spot is the southern side of the river where the old Lugarno ferry use to cross. Once here you will find a number of spots that you can set yourself up for a fish. A short distance downstream you will find a small park that also has a number of deep-water spots that you can fish from.

TACTICS

I would take along a couple of 18.8 to 2.1 metre rods. This way you could set up one with a bait on it and while you are waiting for something to take it you can use either soft plastics or blades on the other one for bream, whiting and flathead.

Try using either a running ball sinker down onto the bait or a running ball sinker down onto the swivel with a long leader.

BAITS AND LURES

Best baits by far for the bream, flathead, flounder and whiting would be blood worms and pink nippers. You could also use pillie tails, strips of mullet and tuna. Chicken breast also goes well here. Great place to work the shoreline with soft plastics and blades, as there are very little snags. Cast out as far as possible and slowly work them back to the shoreline.

BEST TIDE/TIMES

The depth of the water here is deep, but it is a productive spot to chase flathead and bream during the warmer months of the year with soft plastics and strips of mullet during the winter months.

AMENITIES

There is nothing here. You will need to go back to the nearby shops at Illawong.

KIDS AND FAMILIES

Maybe the kids could explore along the shoreline of check out the place for the odd wallaby or two.

GEORGES RIVER NATIONAL PARK

🔍 HOW TO GET THERE

Travel along Henry Lawson Drive until you reach the corner of the River Road. Depending on which way you are coming you will need to turn into the Georges River National Park entrance. Here you will find a gate house, a boat ramp, beach and a road that leads around to where they call Cattle Duffers.

ABOVE: *Plenty of room for the shore-based angler along the stretch of water and up to what they call "Cattle Duffers"..*

LEFT: *Bait fishing with either chicken breast or mullet will produce a few fish here.*

🔍 SNAPSHOT

Platform
ROCK RETAINING WALL
SANDY BEACHES
BOAT RAMP

Target species
BREAM
DUSKY FLATHEAD
SAND WHITING
FLOUNDER
TAILOR
LUDERICK

Best baits
BLOOD WORMS
PINK NIPPERS
WHOLE & HALF PILCHARDS
WHITEBAIT
STRIPS OF MULLET
GREEN WEED
PUDDING BAITS

Best lures
SOFT PLASTICS
SOFT VIBES

Best time
RISING AND FALLING TIDES

SEASONS

Bream **Feb.– May**
Dusky flathead
Nov.– Apr.
Garfish **Year round**
Luderick **Mar.– Sep.**
Mullet **Year round**
Mulloway **Year round**
Sand whiting **Oct.– Apr.**

The only bad thing about fishing from the shoreline here is that you have to pay for the privilege to do so. There are plenty of spots to pull up and cast a line out into deep water. I wouldn't suggest that you go swimming here are there are usually plenty of bull sharks patrolling about.

TACTICS

Maybe take two rods and set one up in a PVC rod holder for whiting and bream, while you work those lures for the flathead and bream that can be caught here. The odd flounder can be caught here during the warmer months.

BAITS AND LURES

Try using pink nippers or blood worms here. If not, I would try squirt or tube worms for whiting, bream and flathead. Great place to have ago with soft plastics and blades as you can cast out wide into deep water. Remember to work them back to where you are standing in small, but slow hops.

BEST TIDE/TIMES

A couple of hours either side of the top of the tides works better when fishing from here. As you can use a shorter rod, because you don't have to cast as far. Early morning or late afternoon or even during the night is ideal for here. When it's raining, you don't seem to get as much pedestrian traffic here during the day.

AMENITIES

As this is a State National Park there is a fee to park and use the area. You could always get a yearly pass that will allow you access to many of the other parks in NSW. Georges River National Park is open from 6am to 7.30pm during daylight savings (6am to 6.30pm at other times) but may have to close at times due to poor weather or fire danger.

KIDS AND FAMILIES

Georges River National Park is a great place for a family daytrip where you can enjoy a picnic or barbecue, go walking or fishing. The landscape of the park includes striking rock formations, steep forested hillsides, plateaus and riverside flats, providing ample opportunities for picnics, barbecues, fishing and walking. If you're interested in birdwatching, be sure to walk the Yeramba Lagoon track.

KELSO BEACH RESERVE

HOW TO GET THERE

Travelling from
the north from the
Milperra Bridge along
Henry Lawson Drive
you will need to stop
opposite Kelso Park
South. Here you will
find off street parking.

SNAPSHOT

Platform
ESTUARY BEACH
MANGROVES

Target species
BREAM
DUSKY FLATHEAD
FLOUNDER, GARFISH
LEATHERJACKETS
LUDERICK, MULLET
MULLOWAY
SAND WHITING

Best baits
BLOOD WORMS
PINK NIPPERS
WHOLE & HALF PILCHARDS
WHITEBAIT
STRIPS OF MULLET
GREEN WEED
PUDDING BAITS

Best lures
SMALL AND LARGE
SOFT PLASTICS
SOFT AND METAL VIBES

Best time
RISING TIDE

SEASONS

Bream **Feb.– May**
Dusky flathead
Nov.– Apr.
Garfish **Year round**
Leatherjacket **Year round**
Flounder **Nov.– Apr.**
Luderick **Mar.– Sep**
Mullet **Year round**
Mulloway
Spring to Autumn
Sand whiting
Year round

ABOVE: *Fish the beach or the rocky outcrop you can see in the distance on either the run-out or run-in tides.*

LEFT: *Bream frequent this spot and you don't need a kayak to get to them while fishing from the beach.*

There is a small beach on the bend of the river that can be very productive at times for bream, whiting and flathead. Just downstream from here is a set of rocks that can be fished on an out-going tide for bream, flathead, whiting and luderick. At certain times of the year you can find green weed in the creek on the opposite side of the main road.

TACTICS
Make sure that you bring along a rod holder so that you can set your outfits up out of the sand while waiting for that next bite. Great place to try out those new soft plastics and lures as there a very few snags.

A few metres downstream you will find a small set of rocks. This is also a great place to set yourself up for mullet, bream, flathead and luderick on the run-out tide.

BAITS AND LURES
Try using pink nippers or blood worms here. If not, I would try squirt or tube worms for whiting, bream and flathead. Great place to have a go with soft plastics and blades as you can cast out wide into deep water. Remember to work them back to where you are standing in small, but slow hops.

BEST TIDE/TIMES
Fishing both the run-in and run-out tides will produce fish here. On the weekends the boat traffic can get a bit hectic here at times. Late afternoon and early mornings seem to be the quietest.

AMENITIES
There are no nearby amenities. You will need to travel back along Henry Lawson Drive to the nearby shops and petrol station.

KIDS AND FAMILIES
Grassed area that leads down to a small sandy beach. I would not go swimming here as shark do patrol this stretch of the river. While the kids are waiting for a bite, they may like to build a sand castle or play in the nearby park.

MILPERRA BRIDGE

HOW TO GET THERE

The Milperra Bridge is located on the south-western corner of Bankstown Airport. Coming in from the west you will be travelling along Newbridge Road and from the east you will be on Milperra Road. As this is a busy intersection you will need to keep an eye out for the limited amount of parking on all sides of the bridge. Access can be gained via a walking track on the eastern side of the bridge.

SNAPSHOT

Platform
ROCK RETAINING WALL
CONCRETE LEDGE

Target species
BREAM, BASS
ESTUARY PERCH
DUSKY FLATHEAD
LUDERICK, MULLET
MULLOWAY
SAND WHITING

Best baits
BLOOD WORMS
PINK NIPPERS
WHOLE & HALF PILCHARDS
WHITEBAIT
STRIPS OF MULLET
GREEN WEED
PUDDING BAITS

Best lures
SOFT PLASTICS, SOFT
AND METAL VIBES

Best time
RISING AND FALLING TIDES

SEASONS

Bream **Feb.– May**
Bass
Warmer months of the year
Estuary Perch
Year round
Dusky flathead
Nov.– Apr.
Luderick **Mar.– Sep.**
Mullet **Year round**
Mulloway **Spring to Autumn**
Sand whiting **Oct.– Apr.**

ABOVE: *Bic Frost with a well-conditioned dusky flathead.*

There is fairly deep water under this bridge that can be accessed from either side of the bridge. Long rods are not need to fish from here, but I would suggest that you up your breaking strain of your line to around seven kilos so that you can lift the fish out or maybe take a long-handled net with you.

TACTICS

You could fish here with two rods. Put the heavier outfit (6 to 10 kilo) into a rod holder with a while pilchard, live mullet or large strip of squid or mullet. While at the same time hold onto the 4 to 6 kilo outfit for bream and flathead.

BAITS AND LURES

Try using pink nippers or blood worms here. If not, I would try squirt or tube worms for whiting, bream and flathead. Great place to have ago with soft plastics and blades as you can cast out wide into deep water. Remember to work them back to where you are standing in small, but slow hops.

BEST TIDE/TIMES

Whether it is a run-out or a run-in tide this spot can produce great catches throughout the day. Tide can run very fast here at times through the middle part of the six hours of the tide change.

AMENITIES

There are a couple of nearby shops, a tackle shop and a garage on the western side, plus a KFC and Hungry Jacks on the eastern side of the bridge.

KIDS AND FAMILIES

Small bush land park on both side of the bridge with a small amount of seating.

LAKEWOOD CITY RESERVE-WORONORA

HOW TO GET THERE

If you are travelling from the west, you will need to get onto the Bangor Bypass and travel east along the River Road. Once you have crossed the new Woronora River bridge you will need to turn left into Linden Street, then left again into Tudar Road. Travel along the road until you come to Washington Drive where you will once again turn left and follows this until you come to Coolidge on your right. Here you will find Lakewood City Reserve.

ABOVE: *It's only a short walk from the parking area at the back of the playing fields to where you can fish. Best fished on a falling tide.*

LEFT: *Lure or bait fishing works well here about an hour either side of the tide.*

SNAPSHOT

Platform
SANDY PATCHES
MANGROVE LINED

Target species
BREAM
DUSKY FLATHEAD
GARFISH, MULLET
MULLOWAY
SAND WHITING
LEATHERJACKETS

Best baits
BLOOD WORMS
PINK NIPPERS
WHOLE & HALF PILCHARDS
WHITEBAIT
STRIPS OF MULLET
GREEN WEED
PUDDING BAITS

Best lures
METAL SLICERS
SOFT PLASTICS,
SOFT VIBES

Best time
RISING TIDE

SEASONS

Bream **Feb.– May**
Dusky flathead
Nov.– Apr.
Garfish **Year round**
Mullet **Year round**
Mulloway
Spring to Autumn
Sand whiting **Oct.– Apr.**

Every suburb needs a great family park, a place where you can take the kids for a day of fun in the sun. For residents of Bonnet Bay in Sydney's south, Lakewood City Reserve is the perfect family park. This small reserve has a number of small sandy/muddy beaches from where you can cast out into deeper water.

TACTICS

This is one of those places where at high tide the water level will be up and in amongst the mangroves, while during the lower tide you will find that you have a small sandy beach to fish from. There are a number of spots dotted along this shoreline that you can fish from.

A rod length between 1.8 to 2.1 metres would be idea from here. Try using a running ball sinker down onto the bait or the running ball sinker down onto the swivel with a long leader.

BAITS AND LURES

Best baits by far for the bream, flathead, flounder and whiting would be blood worms and pink nippers. You could also use pillie tails, strips of mullet and tuna. Chicken breast also goes well here. Great place to work the shoreline with soft plastics and blades, as there are very little snags. Cast out as far as possible and slowly work them back to the shoreline.

BEST TIDE/TIMES

A couple of hours either side of the top of the tide seems to produce more fish, but you should also try near the bottom of the tide. Direct your cast to just over the edge of the weed bed.

AMENITIES

Here you will find soccer fields, a playground, covered picnic areas, BBQ's, tennis courts, plenty of parking and a few nearby shops at Bonnet Bay where you can get a drink or coffee and cake.

KIDS AND FAMILIES

This is a great place to bring the kids for a few hours fishing. If they have had enough you can always have a picnic, kick or throw a ball around, play a bit of tennis or walk to the nearby shops and have a look around.

JANNALI RESERVE BOAT RAMP

🔍 HOW TO GET THERE

If you are travelling from the west, you will need to get onto the Bangor Bypass and travel east along the River Road. Once you have crossed the new Woronora River bridge you will need to turn left into Linden Street, then left again into Tudar Road. Travel along the road until you come to Washington Drive where you will once again turn left and follows this until you come the boat ramp on your right.

🔍 SNAPSHOT

Platform
CONCRETE RETAINING WALL

Target species
BREAM
DUSKY FLATHEAD
LUDERICK
MULLET
SAND WHITING

Best baits
BLOOD WORMS
PINK NIPPERS
HALF PILCHARDS
WHITEBAIT
STRIPS OF MULLET
GREEN WEED
PUDDING BAITS

Best lures
SOFT PLASTICS, SOFT VIBES

Best time
RISING AND FALLING TIDES

SEASONS

Bream **Feb.– May**

Dusky flathead
Nov.– Apr.

Garfish **Year round**

Luderick **Mar.– Sep.**

Mullet **Year round**

Sand whiting **Oct.– Apr.**

ABOVE: *Lachlan and Reily Brown love fishing with their grandad for bream and flathead.*

Nestled in the corner of the river here is a small doubled laned boat ramp. The place is bested fished either early in the morning or late afternoon and during the week, as it can get very busy here at times. A short cast will have you out into the deeper water of the bay. Great place to practice using those soft plastics for dusky flathead.

TACTICS

Fish as light as possible. Great place to berley up mullet and garfish with bread and fish with a very small bobby cork.

BAITS AND LURES

Nippers, blood worms, small crabs, strip of either tuna or mullet. You could also try using half pilchards or whole prawns.

BEST TIDE/TIMES

Best fished at or near the top of the tide. Running ball sinker down onto the bait would be the best if you are using bait. As for lures, I would stick to lightly weighted soft plastics. You could try walking the grassed are at the back of the mangrove and look for the breaks in the mangroves. From here you could cast out into the deeper channel.

AMENITIES

Closet amenities are at the Burnum Burnum boat ramp and 600 metres upstream. Access can be gained by travelling south along Washington Drive.

KIDS AND FAMILIES

Nearby Lakewood City Reserve (downstream) is a great place to bring the kids for a few hours fishing. If they have had enough you can always have a picnic, kick or throw a ball around, play a bit of tennis or walk to the nearby shops and have a look around.

Further upstream you will find a playground, fields, cleaning table and bike track at the Burnum Burnum boat ramp.

THE OLD WORONORA RIVER BRIDGE/WEST

HOW TO GET THERE

It can be a bit tricky getting to the western side of the bridge, but if you miss the turn-off you can always turn around and go back across the new Woronora River bridge and as you come off the bridge you will need to look out for the turn-off on the left that will take you down onto Menai Road that leads down to the old Woronora Bridge.

ABOVE: *Fish here for bream, whiting, mullet and flathead on a falling tide.*

ABOVE: *Waiting for that all-important bite.*

The old Woronora River bridge is nestled underneath the new and much higher Woronora Bridge and it can be a place where record fish are caught. Care does need to be taken when the river is in flood as the water level can rise and over flow into the carpark and surrounding low lying areas. Great place to take the kids when they are just starting out using lures.

TACTICS

Fish as light as the conditions will allow. Cast out wide into the deeper water and towards the base of the pylons of the new bridge on the run-out tide. When the tide is rising cast a lightly weighted bait or soft plastic towards the base of the pylons of the old bridge. Walk to shoreline upstream of the bridge casting out lures for bream flathead and whiting.

BAITS AND LURES

This is a great place to come and learn how to use those soft plastics and blades that you have had gathering dust in your tackle box. It maybe shallow, but it can be very productive during the high parts of the tide.

BEST TIDE/TIMES

Best fished at the top of the tide. Run-in or run-out doesn't seem to matter.

AMENITIES

Nearby Prices Circuit Reserve has parking, playground, playing fields, covered picnic table, cleaning tables and toilets.

KIDS AND FAMILIES

On this side of the river there is a caravan park, shops and a restaurant. On the opposite side, just down-stream of the bridge you will find a playground, fields, cleaning table and bike track at the Burnum Burnum boat ramp.

SNAPSHOT

Platform
CONCRETE RETAINING WALL
SANDY BEACH NEARBY

Target species
BREAM
DUSKY FLATHEAD
GARFISH
LUDERICK
MULLET
SAND WHITING

Best baits
BLOOD WORMS
PINK NIPPERS
HALF PILCHARDS
WHITEBAIT
STRIPS OF MULLET
PUDDING BAITS

Best lures
METAL SLICERS, DIVING AND SINKING HARD BODIED LURES, SOFT PLASTICS, SOFT VIBES

Best time
RISING AND FALLING TIDES

SEASONS

Bream **Feb.– May**

Dusky flathead **Nov.– Apr.**

Garfish **Year round**

Luderick **Mar.– Sep.**

Mullet **Year round**

Sand whiting **Oct.– Apr.**

THE OLD WORONORA RIVER BRIDGE/EAST

HOW TO GET THERE

It can be a bit tricky getting to the eastern side of the bridge, but if you miss the turn-off you can always turn around and go back across the new Woronora River bridge and as you come off the bridge you will need to look out for the turn-off on the left that will take you down onto Menai Road that leads down to the old Woronora Bridge. Proceed onto the eastern side of the bridge and turn off at Prince Edward Park Road, right into Thames Street and then right into Liefey Place.

SNAPSHOT

Platform
CAN BE SLIPPERY
SLOPING ROCKS
WHEN SUBMERGED

Target species
BREAM, BASS
ESTUARY PERCH
DUSKY FLATHEAD
GARFISH, LUDERICK
MULLET, SAND WHITING

Best baits
BLOOD WORMS
PINK NIPPERS
HALF PILCHARDS
WHITEBAIT
STRIPS OF MULLET
GREEN WEED
PUDDING BAITS

Best lures
DIVING HARD BODIED LURES
SOFT PLASTICS, SOFT VIBES

Best time
RISING AND FALLING TIDES

SEASONS
Bream **Feb.– May**
Bass **Cooler months of the year**
Estuary Perch **Year round**
Dusky flathead **Nov.– Apr.**
Garfish **Year round**
Luderick **Mar.– Sep.**
Mullet **Year round**
Sand whiting **Oct.– Apr.**

ABOVE: *There are a great set of cleaning tables directly beside the boat ramp. Fish here at the top of the tide*

LEFT: *Care does need to be taken here when walking the shoreline at low tide as the footing can be a bit slippery, but the end results can be great.*

On either side of the western side of the old bridge there is a sandstone retaining wall that will give you easy access to the river. On the south-western side, you will find a slippery rather rocky area that can be fished the run-out tide.

TACTICS
Fish as light as the conditions will allow. Cast out wide into the deeper water and towards the base of the pylons of the new bridge on the run-out tide. When the tide is rising cast a lightly weighted bait or soft plastic towards the base of the pylons of the old bridge. Walk to shoreline upstream of the bridge casting out lures for bream flathead and whiting.

BAITS AND LURES
This is a great place to come and learn how to use those soft plastics and blades that you have had gathering dust in your tackle box. It maybe shallow, but it can be very productive during the high parts of the tide.

BEST TIDE/TIMES
Best fished at the top of the tide. Run-in or run-out doesn't seem to matter.

AMENITIES
Nearby Prices Circuit Reserve has parking, playground, playing fields, covered picnic table, cleaning tables and toilets.

KIDS AND FAMILIES
On the opposite side of the river there is a caravan park, shops and a restaurant. On this side of the river there a park just down-stream of the bridge you will find a playground, fields, cleaning table and bike track at the Burnum Burnum boat ramp.

PRINCE EDWARD PARK – WORONORA RIVER

HOW TO GET THERE

Travelling west across the new Woronora River bridge you will see a turn-off on the left. Follow this down and across the old Woronora River Bridge. Cross to the other side and then turn right onto Prince Edward Park Road. Keep travelling along here until you reach the Woronora River RSL. On your right, will be the parking area for Prince Edward Park.

ABOVE: *This shot clearly shows you the options that you have when fishing from the shore in Prince Edward Park.*

LEFT: *There are some big dusky flathead that lay in wait her for a well-presented lure or bait.*

SNAPSHOT

Platform
CONCRETE RETAINING WALL
SMALL BEACH AND
TIMBER WALKWAY

Target species
BREAM, BASS
ESTUARY PERCH
DUSKY FLATHEAD
GARFISH, LUDERICK
MULLET
SAND WHITING

Best baits
BLOOD WORMS
PINK NIPPERS
HALF PILCHARDS
WHITEBAIT
STRIPS OF MULLET
GREEN WEED
PUDDING BAITS

Best lures
SINKING AND DIVING
HARD BODIED LURES SOFT
PLASTICS, SOFT VIBES

Best time
RISING AND FALLING TIDES

SEASONS

Bream	**Feb.– May**
Bass	Cooler months of the year
Estuary Perch	
	Year round
Dusky flathead	**Nov.– Apr.**
Garfish	**Year round**
Luderick	**Mar.– Sep.**
Mullet	**Year round**
Sand whiting	**Oct.– Apr.**

s a great place to start your Woronora adventure and offers walking tracks, paths, look-outs and plenty of fishing areas. An unusual feature is its ruggedness which attracts groups and individuals who are looking for a challenging hike over a diverse stretch of land. The Park is home to huge paperbarks, turpentine's and gum trees as well as wallabies, echidnas, sugar gliders and "Eric the Koala" who has been moving between local national parks and reserves for the last decade and is well known too local NPWS officers.

This stretch of shoreline has been done up by fixing the retaining walls and putting in a deck that protrudes out into the deeper part of the river.

TACTICS

This is one of those places where at high tide the water level will be up against the retaining wall. There are a number of spots dotted along this shoreline that you can fish from.

A rod length between 1.8 to 2.1 metres would be idea from here. Try using a running ball sinker down onto the bait or the running ball sinker down onto the swivel with a long leader.

BAITS AND LURES

From the entrance of Loftus Creek entrance and down-stream to the first bend in the river you will be able to pick yourself a spot to set up a couple of chairs so that you can fish in comfort.

BEST TIDE/TIMES

Can be fish during all tides, but seem to produce better fish out wide when the tide is falling. Mullet can be berleyed up on a rising tide.

AMENITIES

Here you will find toilets, a playground, timber wharfs, covered seating and playing fields.

KIDS AND FAMILIES

Great place to bring the kids to explore and fish this terrific section on the Woronora River. If they or you want to explore a bit further upstream you could always cross the bridge and hire a canoe from the Boatshed at Woronora.

Maybe you could also go across the walk across bridge that will take you to the other side of the river where you can take a walking track that leads upstream.

MULLET ROCK

🔍 HOW TO GET THERE

It can be a bit tricky getting to the western side of the bridge, but if you miss the turn-off you can always turn around and go back across the new Woronora River bridge and as you come off the bridge you will need to look out for the turn-off on the left that will take you down onto Menai Road that leads down to the old Woronora Bridge. Before you get to the bridge you will find Prices Circuit. Follows this along until you come to Park Street where you will find limited park. It's just a short walk to Mullet rock beside the walk across bridge.

🔍 SNAPSHOT

Platform
CONCRETE RETAINING WALL

Target species
BREAM, BASS
ESTUARY PERCH
DUSKY FLATHEAD
GARFISH, MULLET
WHITING

Best baits
BLOOD WORMS
PINK NIPPERS
WHITEBAIT
STRIPS OF MULLET
GREEN WEED
PUDDING BAITS

Best lures
METAL SLICERS
SOFT PLASTICS,
SOFT VIBES

Best time
RISING AND FALLING
TIDES

SEASONS

Bream   **Feb.– May**
Bass
Throughout the year
Estuary Perch
Throughout the year
Dusky flathead
Nov.– Apr.
Garfish **Year round**
Mullet **Year round**
Whiting **Oct.– Apr.**

ABOVE: *A couple of anglers using a Kelly Pole and a small float to catch mullet here.*

RIGHT: *Oliver Brown loves his fishing and he managed to get a small bream on his own Okuma outfit.*

There is a small boat ramp situated just under the bridge at the end of Lilyfield Road. This ramp is not much of a ramp, but at high tide you could try casting an unweighted bait out under the bridge. This is a great place to set a poddy trap on a rising tide.

TACTICS
Fish here with a small float for mullet and the odd garfish. You could also try using the running ball sinker down onto the bait when the tide is not running to fast. A sinker down onto a swivel and a long leader when the tide flow picks up.

BAITS AND LURES
Bread and pudding mixtures are great baits. Remember to berley to bring the fish to the base of the rock. For bream, flathead and whiting try blood worms and small strips of mullet or chicken gut.

BEST TIDE/TIMES
Both the run-in and run-out tides fish well here.

AMENITIES
On this side of the river there is not much. You will have to cross the bridge to find toilets, a playground, timber wharfs, covered seating and playing fields on the other side.

KIDS AND FAMILIES
Great place to bring the kids to explore and fish this terrific section on the Woronora River. If they or you want to explore a bit further upstream you could always cross the bridge and hire a canoe from the Boatshed at Woronora.
Maybe you could take a walking track that leads upstream to a couple more land-based spots.

BOAT HARBOUR

HOW TO GET THERE

Travel from Cronulla in the south along Captain Cook Drive until you see the entrance to the Holt's private 4WD area and beach. Here you will need to pay a daily entry fee or get yourself a yearly pass.

ABOVE: *Drummer, luderick, bream and trevally can be berleyed up from the rocks on the northern side of Boat Harbour.*

SNAPSHOT

Platform
OCEAN ROCKS DEEP AND SHALLOW WATER

Target species
BREAM, DART
DRUMMER, GROPER
KINGSFISH
LEATHERJACKETS
LUDERICK
PANED SIZED SNAPPER
YELLOWTAIL
SALMON
SILVER TREVALLY
SQUID, TAILOR
TARWHINE

Best baits
CUNJI, SQUID
WHOLE & HALF PILCHARDS
WHITEBAIT
STRIPS OF MULLET
GREEN WEED
PUDDING BAITS

Best lures
METAL SLICERS
FLOATING DIVING LURES
STICK BAITS
MEDIUM TO LARGE
SURFACE POPPERS

Best time
RISING AND FALLING TIDES

oat Harbour's biggest claim to fame, apart from being the site of many temporary shacks and a 4WD park is a great place to get back to nature. Boat Harbour and the surrounding intertidal rock platforms are a significant part of Kurnell's marine environment. In late 2001, NSW Fisheries announced the establishment of a new Boat Harbour Aquatic Reserve. The new Reserve will place restrictions on fishing and bait collecting in areas next to and adjacent to the Merries Reef area. Boat Harbour is also the location of a 4WD park in which use of Holt's private beach is permitted for a fee.

TACTICS

Use bobby corks to keep the baits off the snaggy bottom. Cast towards the sandy patches with a running ball sinker down onto the bait. Don't forget to take a few squid jigs and 30 to 60gram metal slicers. Five-inch ZMan StreakZ and scented Jerk ShadZ and eight-inch StreakZ XL Jerkbaits on TT Jig heads would be great for working those close in washes.

BAITS AND LURES

Live baits like slimy mackerel, yellowtail and squid

ABOVE: *Scotty Lyons cleaning a nice catch that were caught off the rocks. Peeled prawns, bread for berley and fishing light were the key to his success.*

for kingfish. Peeled prawns, nippers, strips of tuna, mullet, slimy mackerel and squid for most other fish species. Cunje, green weed and cabbage would be good for drummer, luderick and groper.

BEST TIDE/TIMES

The last couple of hours of the rising tide and the first three hours of the falling tide will help your berley attract the fish. Care needs to be taken fishing off the rocks as the swell can come in here without notice. Not a place to fish at night. Best fished throughout the day.

AMENITIES

There are no toilets out here.

KIDS AND FAMILIES

You could walk across the rocks to the beach at boat harbour and go for a swim or you could explore the rock pools. Watch out for blue ringed octopus.

SEASONS

Bream **Feb.– May**
Dart **Year round**
Drummer
Autumn to the end of winter
Groper **Apr.– Sep.**
Kingfish **Nov.– May**
Leatherjackets **Year round**
Paned sized snapper **Winter**
Salmon **Mar.– Jun.**
Silver Trevally **Mar.– Jun.**
Squid **Year round**
Tailor **Mar.– Aug.**
Tarwhine **Feb.– May.**
Yellowtail **Year round**

GREEN HILLS

🔍 HOW TO GET THERE

From Taren Point you will need to travel east along Captain Cook Drive until you reach the round-a-bout at Elouera Road. Proceed on the road for about 50 metres and then turn left into Bate Bay Road. Once at the top of the hill you will see a huge carpark on your left. If you go right to the end and park it will be a short walk across the grass and through a sandy track and onto the beach. The Greenhills section of this long beach is to your left. If you are coming from Cronulla, you can find your way onto Elouera Road and then turn right into Bate Bay Road. From Taren Point you will need to travel east along Captain Cook Drive until you reach the round-a-bout at Elouera Road. Proceed on the road for about 50 metres and then turn left into Bate Bay Road. Once at the top of the hill you will see a huge carpark on your left and one on your right. Wand surf club will be directly in front of you.

ABOVE: *A couple of old timers have set up for their whiting session off Greenhills Beach.*

RIGHT: *When the conditions are calm you won't have to cast out very far to get a few bream, whiting and dart from here.*

🔍 SNAPSHOT

Platform
OCEAN BEACH

Target species
BREAM, DART
MULLOWAY, SALMON
SILVER TREVALLY
TAILOR
TARWHINE

Best baits
BLOOD WORMS,
PINK NIPPERS
WHOLE & HALF PILCHARDS
WHITEBAIT, SQUID
STRIPS OF MULLET
WHOLE YELLOWTAIL

Best lures
METAL SLICERS, SOFT
PLASTICS, SOFT VIBES

Best time
RISING AND FALLING TIDES

SEASONS

Bream **Feb.– May**
Dart **Year round**
Mulloway **Year round**
Salmon **Mar.– Jun.**
Silver Trevally **Mar.– Jun.**
Tailor **Mar.– Aug.**
Tarwhine **Feb.– May**

Greenhills Beach stretches from north Wanda in the south to Boat Harbour in the north. This beach can at times look very uninviting with not many features to it, but this shouldn't stop you from casting a line from it. You will also need to remember that this is a dog off the lease beach and it can get very crowed on the weekends.

TACTICS

Direct your cast towards the edges of the deep gutters You could also try casting up onto the sand banks and letting the flow of the water bring you baits back down over the edge of the drop-offs.

BAITS AND LURES

If you find that the tailor and salmon are feeding too far out for your baits, try using 40 to 70gram metal slicers for those hard to fish. Whole pilchards and garfish on ganged hooks would be the go. Beach and blood worms, nippers and half pilchards would be good for bream, trevally, dart and tarwhine.

BEST TIDE/TIMES

This will depend on the types of gutters that have formed here at the time of your visit. Early morning, late afternoon or at night seems to produce the better catches. Overcast days do fire at times.

AMENITIES

The closest toilets and showers would be at the Wanda Surf Club.

KIDS AND FAMILIES

The stretch of beach is not patrolled. If you were going for a swim, I would suggest that you go back to the Flags in front of the Wanda Surf Club. The kids could kick and throw a ball on the beach or dig with their feet for pipis.

WANDA BEACH

HOW TO GET THERE

From Taren Point you will need to travel east along Captain Cook Drive until you reach the round-a-bout at Elouera Road. Proceed on the road for about 50 metres and then turn left into Bate Bay Road. Once at the top of the hill you will see a huge carpark on your left. If you go right to the end and park it will be a short walk across the grass and through a sandy track and onto the beach. The Greenhills section of this long beach is to your left. If you are coming from Cronulla, you can find your way onto Elouera Road and then turn right into Bate Bay Road. From Taren Point you will need to travel east along Captain Cook Drive until you reach the round-a-bout at Elouera Road. Proceed on the road for about 50 metres and then turn left into Bate Bay Road. Once at the top of the hill you will see a huge carpark on your left and one on your right. Wand surf club will be directly in front of you.

ABOVE: *Beach and tube worms are the go when targeting whiting off the beach. Pink nippers would be the next best bait.*

RIGHT: *A couple of anglers are working the falling tide for a few beach worms.*

SNAPSHOT

Platform
OCEAN BEACH

Target species
BREAM, DART
MULLOWAY
SALMON
SILVER TREVALLY
TAILOR, TARWHINE

Best baits
BLOOD WORMS
PINK NIPPERS
WHOLE & HALF PILCHARDS
WHITEBAIT
STRIPS OF MULLET
SQUID
WHOLE YELLOWTAIL

Best lures
METAL SLICERS
SOFT PLASTICS,
SOFT VIBES

Best time
RISING AND FALLING TIDES

SEASONS

Bream **Feb.– May**
Dart **Year round**
Mulloway **Year round**
Salmon **Mar.– Jun.**
Silver Trevally **Mar. – Jun.**
Tailor **Mar.– Aug.**
Tarwhine **Feb.– May**

Wanda is the furthest patrolled beach north on the Cronulla stretch. It is a sand beach and a may have a smaller crowd due to its location. There is kiosk which is open in the summer months. Cleared areas of Wanda Reserve just behind the beach and nearby Don Lucas Reserve are dog on-leash areas. Greenhills Beach, located north of Wanda (north of Track 5), contains a dog off-leash area at designated times, which is popular with walkers.

TACTICS

Direct your cast towards the edges of the deep gutters You could also try casting up onto the sand banks and letting the flow of the water bring you baits back down over the edge of the drop-offs.

BAITS AND LURES

If you find that the tailor and salmon are feeding too far out for your baits, try using 40 to 70gram metal slicers for those hard to fish. Whole pilchards and garfish on ganged hooks would be the go. Beach and blood worms, nippers and half pilchards would be good for bream, trevally, dart and tarwhine. Have ago at getting your own beach worms or buying them at Macs Bait Bar Blakehurst.

BEST TIDE/TIMES

This will depend on the types of gutters that have formed here at the time of your visit. Early morning, late afternoon or at night seems to produce the better catches. Overcast days do fire at times.

AMENITIES

The surf club has toilets, change rooms and showers.

KIDS AND FAMILIES

There is a nearby playground and walking tracks. You could go swimming between the flags in front of the club.

CRONULLA POINT

🔍 HOW TO GET THERE

From Miranda, you will need to travel east along the Kingsway until you reach the junction at Elouera Road. Drive down Ewos Parade and find a parking spot somewhere. Then walk through one of the many side streets to Cronulla Point. Or you could park in the south Cronulla Carpark and walk along the esplanade to the point.

🔍 SNAPSHOT

Platform
OCEAN ROCK

Target species
BREAM
DRUMMER
GROPER
KINGFISH
LEATHERJACKETS
SALMON
SILVER TREVALLY
SQUID
TAILOR

Best baits
WHOLE & HALF PILCHARDS
GARFISH, SQUID
PRAWNS, CABBAGE
GREEN WEED

Best lures
METAL SLICERS
STICK BAITS &
SURFACE LURES

Best time
FISH DURING SMALL
SWELL, FALLING TIDE

SEASONS

Bream **Feb.– May**
Drummer
Autumn to the end of winter
Groper **Apr.– Sep.**
Kingfish **Nov.– May**
Leatherjacket **Year round**
Salmon **Mar.– Jun.**
Silver Trevally **Mar.– Jun.**
Squid **Year round**
Tailor **Mar.– Aug.**

ABOVE: *It's only a short walk from the promenade at South Cronulla to a great little spot at the famous Cronulla Point. Fish as light as the conditions will allow here.*

TOP: *This larger squid fell to a carefully worked Fish Inc squid jig.*

Cronulla Point is mainly known for its right-hand break that at time can get to five metres. Now if you are an angler you will see another side to the point as there are large boulders, kelp, weed and in close to the corner there is a mixture of sand and broken shells on the bottom. If you prefer not to fish off the rocks, there is always the southern and northern corners of the beach. This is a great place to fish during the cooler months of the year when the beach is not patrolled.

TACTICS

During the lower tides, it would be a good idea to fish with a bait suspended underneath a bobby cork or used a 3 to 3.6 metre outfit to cast out wide onto the sand. The suggested rig is the paternoster, as it will help you get away from the snags.

BAITS AND LURES

Whole pilchards and garfish rigged on a set of ganged hooks. Prawns, pillie tails, strips of tuna and mullet, cunje and bread would be ideal for bait. Berley with chopped up old pilchards, bread and chicken pellets. Don't forget to take a few squid jig and 40 to 70gram metal slicers.

BEST TIDE/TIMES

Fish here at all tides. You will need to watch the swell here, as it is very exposed. Good in a southerly, not good in a northerly.

AMENITIES

Toilets, change rooms and showers are in the nearby South Cronulla surf lifesaving club. There are also public toilets next to the club.

KIDS AND FAMILIES

Patrolled beach, grassed area and kiddie's playground can be found here. When you tire of fishing you could always take a walk along the Esplanade south to Shelly Beach and Windy Point.

WINDY POINT

HOW TO GET THERE

From Miranda, you will need to travel east along the Kingsway until you reach the junction at Elouera Road. Drive down Ewos Parade and continue on to Orient Avenue. Park here and then walk through to the Esplanade. Look to your left and you will see Windy Point.

SNAPSHOT

Platform
OCEAN ROCK

Target species
BREAM, DRUMMER GROPER, KINGFISH LEATHERJACKETS LUDERICK PANED SIZED SNAPPER SALMON SILVER TREVALLY SQUID, TAILOR TARWHINE YELLOWTAIL

Best baits
WHOLE & HALF PILCHARDS GARFISH, SQUID, PRAWNS CABBAGE, GREEN WEED

Best lures
METAL SLICERS STICK BAITS & SURFACE LURES

Best time
FISH DURING SMALL SWELL, FALLING TIDE

ABOVE: *South of Windy Point can be fished in slight seas for drummer, bream and trevally.*

TOP RIGHT: *A couple of anglers waiting for that early morning bite while fishing the washes.*

BOTTOM RIGHT: *Bill Lyons with a kilo plus bream caught while fishing with peeled prawns near Windy Point.*

I have no idea where the name Windy Point comes from, perhaps because to fish here you need calm seas, normally present when there are strong westerly winds. On the south-eastern side a decent cast will get you out to a number of sandy patches. The north-western side has a fair amount of protection from the southerly winds, but once again a decent cast is needed.

TACTICS

During the lower tides, it would be a good idea to fish with a bait suspended underneath a bobby cork or used a 3 to 3.6 metre outfit to cast out wide onto the sand. The suggested rig is the paternoster, as it will help you get away from the snags.

BAITS AND LURES

Whole pilchards and garfish rigged on a set of ganged hooks. Prawns, pillie tails, strips of tuna and mullet, cunje and bread would be ideal for bait. Berley with chopped up old pilchards, bread and chicken pellets. Don't forget to take a few squid jig and 40 to 70gram metal slicers.

BEST TIDE/TIMES

Fish here at all tides. You will need to watch the swell here, as it is very exposed. Good in a southerly, not good in a northerly.

AMENITIES

Nearby Shelly Park has toilets, change rooms and showers.

KIDS AND FAMILIES

Ocean swimming pool, park and kid's playground are nearby at Shelly Park. There is also a restaurant and café nearby.

SEASONS

Bream	**Feb.– May**
Drummer	
Autumn to the end of winter	
Groper	**Apr.– Sep.**
Kingfish	**Nov.– May**
Leatherjackets	**Year round**
Luderick	**Mar.– Sep.**
Paned sized Snapper	**Winter**
Salmon	**Mar.– Jun.**
Silver Trevally	**Mar.– Jun.**
Squid	**Year round**
Tailor	**Mar.– Aug.**
Tarwhine	**Feb.– May**
Tellowtail	**Year round**

DAROOK PARK

🔍 HOW TO GET THERE

Travel east along President Avenue from Sutherland and then continue along the Kingsway at Caringbah until you reach Cronulla. Turn off at Willbar Avenue and then into Cronulla Street. Follow this along until you come to Nicholson Parade. Keep travelling south until you find Darook Park on your right.

🔍 SNAPSHOT

Platform
BEACH AND ROCKY POINTS

Target species
BREAM
FLATHEAD
SALMON
SILVER TREVALLY
SQUID
TAILOR
WHITING

Best baits
PINK NIPPER
WORMS, PRAWNS.

Best lures
SMALL META SLICERS,
SMALL SURFACE POPPERS
STICK BAITS &
SURFACE LURES

Best time
EITHER SIDE OF THE
TOP OF THE TIDE

ABOVE: *When the tide is high you can work those surface lures right from the shore and as the tide falls follow the receding tide to the drop-off.*

RIGHT: *Try walking the flats either lure or bait fishing at Darook Park for trevally, as Andrew Humphries did.*

SEASONS

Bream **Feb.– May**
Dusky flathead
Year round
Salmon **Mar.– Jun.**
Silver Trevally **Mar.– Jun.**
Squid **Year round**
Tailor **Mar.– Aug.**
Whiting **Year round**

Darook Park has a northern and southern end and is one of those hidden gems in Cronulla where you can while away the hours just watching the world go by. There is a small sandy beach that is washed by the movement of the tide in the beautiful Port Hacking River.

TACTICS

If you are going to fish here during the higher tides you will need to be prepared to get wet as the depth can be waist deep. If you start fishing at the top of the tide at the water's edge and as the tide recedes you will work your way out to the drop-off into deeper water. I carry all my gear in a shoulder bag and just use one rod.

BAITS AND LURES

Great place to use surface lures for bream flathead and whiting. Half pilchards, prawns, nippers and blood worms would be great here.

BEST TIDE/TIMES

Fish from a quarter of the tide down to the bottom and then back up.

AMENITIES

Toilets and disabled access.

KIDS AND FAMILIES

Great place to come when the wind direction is from the north and it is a very popular swimming place.

GUNNAMATTA BAY BATHS

HOW TO GET THERE

Travel east along President Avenue from Sutherland and then continue along the Kingsway at Caringbah until you reach Cronulla. Turn off at Willbar Avenue and then into Cronulla Street. Follow this along until you come to Nicholson Parade. There is plenty of parking beside Gunnamatta Park. Then all you need to do is walk through the park to the baths.

ABOVE: *Great place to get to get your live squid, yellowtail and slimy mackerel. While you are there you should also set a line for bream, whiting and flathead.*

RIGHT: *You don't have to have a rod to fish from here. A handline will do the job.*

The Gunnamatta Bay Baths are situated on the shoreline of the Gunnamatta Bay Park, where you will find plenty of things to do with family and friends other than fishing. The adjacent park has a large grassy slope that provides lots of open space for everyone to spread out under the shade provided by the large native trees.

TACTICS

You can try lure fishing from here for dusky flathead, whiting and bream a couple of hours either side of the top of the tide.

BAITS AND LURES

Half or whole pilchards, garfish, prawns, nipper, blood and beach worms are the go here. During the cooler months of the year you could try using strips of mullet, tuna, bonito or chicken gut. Don't forget to take along a few 30 to 50-gram metal slicers for the tailor and salmon. Great place to work those soft plastics and blades for flathead.

BEST TIDE/TIMES

Can be fished day or night and right through the tide.

AMENITIES

Toilets, showers, change rooms and covered picnic areas are nearby in the park.

KIDS AND FAMILIES

Great place to bring the family for a swim in the tidal netted pool, have a picnic, play in the sand and have a fish.

SNAPSHOT

Platform
MAN MADE TIMBER AND CONCRETE STRUCTURE

Target species
BREAM, KINGFISH
LEATHERJACKETS
LUDERICK
SALMON
SILVER TREVALLY
SQUID, TAILOR
TARWHINE
YELLOWTAIL

Best baits
WHOLE & HALF PILCHARDS
GARFISH, SQUID, PRAWNS
CABBAGE, GREEN WEED

Best lures
METAL SLICES
STICK BAITS &
SURFACE LURES

Best time
RISING AND
FALLING TIDES

SEASONS

Bream	**Feb.– May**
Kingfish	**Nov.– May**
Leatherjackets	**Year round**
Luderick	**Mar.– Sep.**
Salmon	**Mar.– Jun.**
Silver Trevally	**Mar.– Jun.**
Squid	**Year round**
Tailor	**Mar.– Aug.**
Tarwhine	**Feb.– May**
Yellowtail	**Year round**

TONKIN PARK

Travel east along President Avenue from Sutherland and then continue along the Kingsway at Caringbah until you reach Cronulla. Just before the start of the shops at Cronulla you will need to turn right into Wilbar Avenue. Proceed to the round-a-bout and go underneath the train line. Tonkin Park will be on your left. Or you could continue along Wilbar Avenue and then into Cronulla Street. Once you have gone past the railway station you will need to turn right into Nicholson Parade, then directly into Tonkin Street. At the end of the street you will find a small parking area adjacent to the boat ramp.

🔍 SNAPSHOT

Platform
MAN MADE ROCK RETAINING WALL WITH PATHWAY

Target species
BREAM
DUSKY FLATHEAD
GARFISH
MULLET

Best baits
FILLET OR PILCHARD GARFISH, PRAWNS BREAD PUDDING BAITS

Best lures
METAL SLICERS
STICK BAITS &
SURFACE LURES

Best time
EITHER SIDE OF THE TOP OF THE TIDE

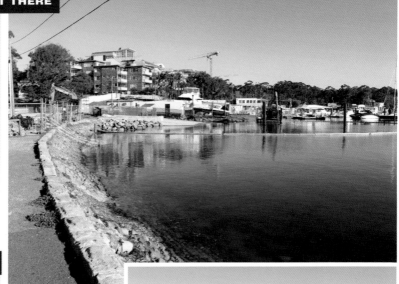

ABOVE: *A new boat ramp and pontoon is being installed at the end of Gunnamatta Bay.*

RIGHT: *A couple of anglers fishing the small drain at high tide for bream, mullet, whiting and flathead.*

SEASONS

Bream **Feb.– May**
Dusky flathead
Warmer months
Garfish **Year round**
Mullet **Year round**

Nestled in the back of Gunnamatta Bay you will find a small, shallow one-laned boat ramp with limited parking. The park is mainly used for sporting activities, plus the occasional fair. What is great about this spot is that the wall end of the bay is a great and safe place to cast a bait or work those lures you have.

TACTICS

Use a small float or try using soft plastics here.

BAITS AND LURES

Fish with a float for mullet and garfish. Small ball sinker down onto the bait for bream and soft plastics for the flathead.

BEST TIDE/TIMES

Best fished during the top part of the tides as it is very shallow here. You could walk out to near the edge of the drop-off, but you are going to need a good pair of shoes to protect your feet.

AMENITIES

Toilets are nearby in the parking area.

KIDS AND FAMILIES

Oval nearby, short walk to the shops and there is a marina and coffee shop on the opposite side of the boat ramp.

WATER STREET BOAT RAMP

HOW TO GET THERE 🔍

Travel east along President Avenue from Sutherland and then continue along the Kingsway at Caringbah. After the set of lights at the top of the hill at Caringbah you will need to turn right into Gannons Road South. Water Street will be about one and a half kilometres down on your right-hand side.

ABOVE: *When fishing at the Water Street ramp at low tide you will need to cast out into the deeper water.*

RIGHT: *This small area at the back of Burraneer Bay can be fished at any tide. Whether you are bait or lure fishing.*

SNAPSHOT 🔍

Platform
BOAT RAMP
SMALL RETAINING WALL
SMALL BEACH AT LOWER TIDES

Target species
BREAM, SQUID
DUSKY FLATHEAD
LEATHERJACKETS
LUDERICK , MULLET
SILVER TREVALLY

Best baits
HALF PILCHARDS
GARFISH, PRAWNS
BREAD, PUDDING BAITS

Best lures
METAL SLICERS, STICK BAITS, SURFACE LURES SHALLOW AND DEEP DIVING LURES

Best time
EITHER SIDE OF THE TOP OF THE TIDE

SEASONS

Bream **Feb.– May**
Dusky flathead **Year round**
Leatherjacket **Year round**
Luderick **Mar.– Sep.**
Mullet **Year round**
Silver Trevally **Mar.– Jun.**
Squid **Year round**

There is not a lot down at the end of Water Street, except for a boat ramp. The area at the end of the ramp has a small sand flat to the left and deep water out in front.

TACTICS

Great place to try out those soft plastics like 3-inch gulp shrimps and ZMan GrubZ. If you are after leatherjackets, I would try using a single hook paternoster rig and either a small piece of peeled prawn or squid for bait.

BAITS AND LURES

Float fish for mullet, luderick and garfish. Make sure that you use some kind of berley.

BEST TIDE/TIMES

Run-out or run-in it doesn't seem to matter as the water depth is fairly deep out wide. There is a shallow sand bank on the left-hand side of the ramp.

AMENITIES

None you will have to go to nearby Gannons Road.

KIDS AND FAMILIES

Not much else to do here other than fish and launch and retrieve a boat.

DOYLANS BAY BOAT RAMP

🔍 HOW TO GET THERE

Travel east along President Avenue from Sutherland and then continue along the Kingsway at Caringbah. At the set of lights at the top of the hill at Caringbah you will need to turn right into Port Hacking Road. Continue on for about three kilometres and veer off left into Port Hacking Road South until you reach the ramp at the bottom of the hill.

🔍 SNAPSHOT

Platform
BOAT RAMP WITH PONTOON

Target species
BREAM, KINGFISH
LEATHERJACKETS
LUDERICK
PANED SIZED SNAPPER
SALMON
SILVER TREVALLY
SQUID, TAILOR
TARWHINE, YELLOWTAIL

Best baits
HALF PILCHARDS
GARFISH, SQUID,
PRAWNS, CABBAGE
GREEN WEED

Best lures
METAL SLICERS STICK
BAITS & SURFACE LURES

Best time
RISING AND FALLING
TIDES

ABOVE: *You can fish off the pontoon for squid, bream, trevally and luderick, but care needs to be taken as it can be very busy at times.*

ABOVE: *Don't forget to take along a few squid jigs when fishing here, as there are usually a few squid about.*

SEASONS
Bream **Feb.– May**
Kingfish **Nov.– May.**
Latherjackets **Year round**
Luderick **Mar.– Sep.**
Paned sized snapper **Winter**
Salmon **Mar.– Jun.**
Silver Trevally **Mar.– Jun.**
Squid **Year round**
Tailor **Mar.– Aug.**
Tarwhine **Feb.– May**
Yellowtail **Year round**

This is predominately a two-lane boat ramp with a very deep drop-off with an adjacent walkway and a floating pontoon. It I s a great place to come for a fish when the wind is coming from a southerly or westerly direction as it faces due north.

TACTICS
You can try lure fishing from here for dusky flathead, whiting and bream a couple of hours either side of the top of the tide. Great place to chase a few squid and yellowtail for live bait.

BAITS AND LURES
Half or whole pilchards, garfish, prawns, nipper, blood and beach worms are the go here. During the cooler months of the year you could try using strips of mullet, tuna, bonito or chicken gut. Don't forget to take along a few 30 to 50-gram metal slicers for the tailor and salmon. Great place to work those soft plastics and blades for flathead.

BEST TIDE/TIMES
Can be fished day or night and right through the tide.

AMENITIES
There are toilets adjacent to the ramp as well as fresh tap water.

KIDS AND FAMILIES
Great place to bring the kids to dangle a line off the floating pontoon.

LILLY PILLY BATHS

HOW TO GET THERE

Travel east along President Avenue from Sutherland and then continue along the Kingsway at Caringbah. At the set of lights at the top of the hill at Caringbah you will need to turn right into Port Hacking Road. Continue on for about three kilometres and veer off to the right into Lilly Pilly Point Road. At the bottom of the road you will find an access road that will lead to the baths. Check opening and closing times of the gate.

ABOVE: *Lilly Pilly Baths produces kingfish, salmon, tailor, bream, whiting and flathead.*

RIGHT: *The Lilly Pilly baths is a land-based hot spot in the Port Hacking for kingfish during the warmer months of the year.*

SNAPSHOT

Platform
MAN MADE TIMBER AND CONCRETE STRUCTURE

Target species
BREAM, KINGSFISH
LEATHERJACKETS
LUDERICK
PANED SIZED SNAPPER
SALMON
SILVER TREVALLY
SQUID, TAILOR
TARWHINE
YELLOWTAIL

Best baits
WHOLE & HALF PILCHARDS
GARFISH, SQUID, PRAWN
CABBAGE, GREEM WEED

Best lures
METAL SLICES, STICK
BAITS & SURFACE LURES

Best time
RISING AND FALLING TIDES

Lilli Pilly baths is nestled on the western side of the point at Lilly Pilly and is very popular with anglers who like to target salmon, tailor and kingfish.

TACTICS

Fish out wide for kingfish, tailor and salmon under a bobby cork or try using 30 to 60gram metal slicers. Flathead, whiting, sliver trevally and bream can be caught out wide. Watch out for passing boats. Fish in close for yellowtail, mullet and leatherjackets. You will also need a long handle net.

BAITS AND LURES

Peeled prawns, nipper, blood worms, chicken gut, chicken breast, strips of mullet and tuna, whole pilchards and garfish can be used here. Don't forget 30 to 60gram slicers and squid jigs.

BEST TIDE/TIMES

The run-in or run-out tides both produce fish. It does run fast here at times.

AMENITIES

Toilets are adjacent to the wharf and baths.

KIDS AND FAMILIES

Go for a swim in the tidal pool. Best times are when the tide is high. Watch out for oysters and rocks on the bottom.

SEASONS

Bream **Feb.– May**
Kingfish **Nov.– May**
Leatherjackets **Year round**
Luderick **Mar.– Sep.**
Paned sized snapper **Winter**
Salmon **Mar.– Jun.**
Silver Trevally **Mar.– Jun.**
Squid **Year round**
Tailor **Mar.– Aug.**
Taewhine **Feb.– May**
Yellowtail **Year round**

HOW TO GET THERE

When travelling either north or south along the Prices Highway you will need to turn into the Kingsway. Once you reach the centre of Miranda you will need to turn into Kora Road and travel south until you find Wonga Road, which will be on your left-hand side. As there is limited parking here you may have to walk a short distance to the waters' edge.

SNAPSHOT

Platform
BOAT RAMP, PONTOON
CONCRETE RETAINING WALL

Target species
BREAM
KINGFISH
LEATHERJACKETS
LUDERICK
SILVER TREVALLY
SQUID
TAILOR
YELLOWTAIL
DUSKY FLATHEAD

Best baits
WHOLE & HALF PILCHARDS
GARFISH, SQUID, PRAWNS
CANNAGE, GREEN WEED

Best lures
METAL SLICERS, STICK
BAITS & SURFACE LURES

Best time
RISING AND FALLING TIDES

ABOVE: *Nice sized tailor frequent the wharf at Yowie Bay, so remember to take those small metal lures.*

RIGHT: *Glenn Loveday found that if you use berley while fishing at the Yowie Bay ramp during the quiter times of the day it seems to produce the better results.*

SEASONS

Bream **Feb.– May**

Kingfish **Nov.– May**

Leatherjackets **Year round**

Luderick **Mar.– Sep.**

Silver trevally **Mar.– Jun.**

Squid **Year round**

Tailor **Mar.– Aug.**

Yellowtail **Year round**

At the end of Wonga Road at Yowie Bay you will find a two laned boat ramp with a floating pontoon, concrete retaining wall and an adjacent marina. The water depth here drops off to about nine metres. This area can be very busy at times due to construction workers using the ramp to load and off-load materials.

TACTICS

Try using a small ball sinker down onto the bait and cast it out towards the marina on your left-hand side. Float fishing for luderick is worth a shot here on the run-out tide.

Leatherjackets can be caught on a paternoster rig while using small pieces of squid and peeled prawns.

BAITS AND LURES

Peeled prawns for the leatherjackets, bread for the mullet and garfish, pink nippers and blood worms for the bream and half pilchards and soft plastics for the dusky flathead.

BEST TIDE/TIMES

As this is a very busy boat ramp you will need to pick your times when you come here. Night fishing seems to produce more fish and it is a great place to come for squid, yellowtail and mullet.

AMENITIES

There are nearby toilets, bottle shop, limited single car parking and a small grassed area nearby.

KIDS AND FAMILIES

This is a great place to bring the kids, so that they can dangle a line off the pontoon. Many of the locals will feed the fish here, so it would be a great idea to bring along some bread to feed the fish. Care does need to be taken as this is a very popular ramp.

GYMEA BAY BATHS

HOW TO GET THERE 🔍

When travelling either north or south along the Prices Highway you will need to turn into the Kingsway. Once you reach the lights at Gymea Bay Road south you will turn right and follow this road across President Avenue down to Ellesmere Road. One the bend you will find a small un marked road that you can careful travel down to a small parking area. From here it's a short downhill walk to the baths.

ABOVE: *To get to the baths it's just a short walk from the parking area just up the hill.*

RIGHT: *Angler wait in anticipation for that bite from a kingfish, salmon, tailor or bream that frequent this area.*

SNAPSHOT 🔍

Platform
MAN MADE TIMBER AND CONCRETE STRUCTURE

Target species
DUSKY FLATHEAD KINGFISH, BREAM LEATHERJACKETS LUDERICK, SALMON PANED SIZED SNAPPER SILVER TREVELLY SQUID, TAILOR YELLOWTAIL

Best baits
WHOLE & HALF PILCHARDS GARFISH, SQUID, PRAWNS CABBAGE, GREEN WEED

Best lures
METAL SLICERS, STICK BAITS & SURFACE LURES

Best time
RISING AND FALLING TIDES

This set of tidal baths is nestled in the corner of Gymea Bay and in the early morning you will be looking directly into the sun. The afternoons during winter can turn very cool once the sun has gone down behind the hill.

TACTICS

Fish out wide for kingfish, tailor and salmon under a bobby cork or try using 30 to 60gram metal slicers. Flathead, whiting, sliver trevally and bream can be caught out wide. Watch out for passing boats. Fish in close for yellowtail, mullet and leatherjackets. You will also need a long handle net.

BAITS AND LURES

Peeled prawns, nipper, blood worms, chicken gut, chicken breast, strips of mullet and tuna, whole pilchards and garfish can be used here. Don't forget 30 to 60gram slicers and squid jigs.

BEST TIDE/TIMES

Day or night. It can get quite hot here during the summer months and very cold during the winter in the afternoon.

AMENITIES

Here you will find a tidal netted swimming baths that has a timber wharf on two sides. There is a small parking area halfway down the road and there are nearby toilets. Further up the road this is a corner shop.

KIDS AND FAMILIES

Great place to bring the kids for a fish off the wharf. You could also go for a swim at high tide, but watch out for the rocks and oysters that are in the tidal pool.

SEASONS

Bream **Feb.– May**
Dusky flathead **Year round**
Kingfish **Nov.– May**
Leatherjackets **Year round**
Luderick **Mar.– Sep.**
Paned sized snapper **Winter**
Salmon **Mar– Jun.**
Silver trevally **Mar.– Jun.**
Tailor **Mar.– Aug.**
Yellowtail **Year round**

GRAYS POINT FLATS

🔍 HOW TO GET THERE

When travelling either north or south along the Prices Highway you will need to turn into the Kingsway. Then turn right at the first set of lights and continue along Clements Road and go over the rail bridge into Hotham Avenue. Cross over President avenue into North West Arm Road and wind your way through Grays Point down to a set of shops. Continue through to Manson Road where you will park and then take a short walk to the bottom where you will find a set of sand flats at low tide.

🔍 SNAPSHOT

Platform
SAND BEACH DURING THE LOWER PARTS OF THE TIDE

Target species
BREAM
DUSKY FLATHEAD
SILVER TREVALLY
TAILOR
WHITING

Best baits
HALF PILCHARDS
GARFISH
PRAWNS
BREAD
PUDDING BAITS

Best lures
METAL SLICERS,
SMALL STICK BAITS
& SURFACE LURES

Best time
RISING AND FALLING TIDES

SEASONS

Bream **Feb.– May**
Dusky flathead
Year round
Silver trevally **Mar.– Jun.**
Tailor **Mar.– Aug.**
Whiting **Year round**

ABOVE: *The author cast out a few so plastics here during the last hour of the run-out tide*

LEFT: *Work those Atomic hard-bodied lures over the sand flats from high tide and down to the drop-off in the channel.*

At the end of the road there is a carpark from where you can walk down a short track to the water where you will find a set of sand flats will be covered most of the time. Good place to pump for nippers as the tide is falling or as it starts to come back up.

TACTICS

Try fishing as the tide recedes and work your way out to the drop-off into the channel. Fish on the downstream side of the flats as the tide runs out and as the tide rises you should try the upstream side of the flats. Try surface fishing at the top of the tie for whiting, bream and flathead.

BAITS AND LURES

Peeled prawns, nipper, blood worms, chicken gut, chicken breast, strips of mullet and tuna, whole pilchards and garfish can be used here. Don't forget 30 slicers and those soft plastics, blades and hard bodied lures for the flathead and bream.

BEST TIDE/TIMES

Low or high tide.

AMENITIES

Toilets, BBQ's, covered picnic tables and a grassed are can be found back at Swallow Rock Drive boat ramp.

KIDS AND FAMILIES

Small bush area near the carpark.

SWALLOW ROCK DRIVE RESERVE

HOW TO GET THERE

When travelling either north or south along the Prices Highway you will need to turn into the Kingsway. Then turn right at the first set of lights and continue along Clements Road and go over the rail bridge into Hotham Avenue. Cross over President avenue into North West Arm Road and wind your way through Grays Point down to a set of shops. Turn right into Swallow Rock Drive and make yourself down the waters' edge.

ABOVE: *As this area has a boat ramp, it can get very busy at times. So fishing is at its best during the quiter times of the day or night.*

LEFT: *Try either fishing off the pontoon or the nearby beach for whiting, flathead and bream.*

SNAPSHOT

Platform
BOAT RAMP WITH PONTOON AND SANDY BEACH

Target species
BREAM
DUSKY FLATHEAD
GARFISH
LUDERICK
MULLET

Best baits
HALF PILCHARDS
GARFISH, SQUID,
PRAWNS, CABBAGE
GREEN WEED

Best lures
METAL SLICERS,
SMALL STICK BAITS &
SURFACE LURES

Best time
RISING AND FALLING TIDES

This is a well-kept area that is a great place to bring the family for an outing, as they can watch other anglers launch and retrieve their boats, while at the same time have a fish from the shore.

TACTICS

On the downstream side of the ramp there are some mangroves that leads to a rocky point. You can fish from here or the beach. Watch out for the boat traffic. On the upstream side of the ramp there is a beach that stretches to another rocky point. Luderick can be caught off this point. Cast out wide with your baits for bream. Fish form the beach with soft plastics for dusky flathead. Mullet and garfish can be berleyed up in close with bread.

BAITS AND LURES

Try those ZMan 3-inch scented Podyz and Minnowz, 4-inch Diezel Minnowz and Swimmerz soft plastics, plus Gulp 4-inch Nemesis and Grubs. Best baits by far are pink nipper and blood worms. You could also try using chicken breast and mullet strips. Green weed for the luderick and bread for the mullet and garfish.

BEST TIDE/TIMES

Best fished at when the tide is half tide to full and about half way down. Fairly shallow in close with a bit deeper water out further.

AMENITIES

Nearby toilets, BBQ's covered seating, grassed area, beach and small playground.

KIDS AND FAMILIES

Great place to bring the family and friends for a BBQ or picnic where you can also go for a fish.

SEASONS

Bream **Feb.– May**
Dusky Flathead **Year round**
Garfish **Year round**
Garfish **Year round**
Luderick **Mar.– Sep.**
Mullet **Year round**

HOW TO GET THERE

Whether you are travelling form the north or up from the south along the Prince Highway you will need to turn at the set of lights at Farnell Avenue that leads to the entrance to the Royal National Park. There is a fee to park your car when using the RNP. This can be paid at the shop at Audley. Work your way down the road and before you travel across the weir at Audley you will need to turn left into Riverside Road. There are a couple of carparks along this road for you to stop at before you get to Reid's Flat. Park fee applies if you are going to park your car here.

SNAPSHOT

Platform
SANDY BEACH, ROCK RETAINING WALLS

Target species
BASS
BREAM
DUSKY FLATHEAD
GARFISH
LUDERICK
MULLET

Best baits
HALF PILCHARDS
GARFISH, SQUID, WORMS, PINK NIPPERS, PRAWNS
BREAD PUDDING BAITS

Best lures
SMALL STICK BAITS & SURFACE LURES, SOFT PLASTICS AND VIBES

Best time
RISING AND FALLING TIDES

SEASONS

Bass
Warmer months of the year

Bream **Feb.– May**

Dusky flathead
Year round

Garfish **Year round**

Luderick **Mar.– Sep.**

Mullet **Year round**

ABOVE: *There is a small area of flats here that can be fished right through the tide. Great place to take the kids.*

If you are going to fish off the shore at Reid's Flat you will need to remember that you are in the RNP and you will have to either have a daily pass or a yearly one. At the end of the narrow road that leads to a vast picnic area you will plenty of places that you can fish from.

TACTICS

Cast ZMan and Berkley Powerbaits from the rock wall out into the deep water and work them back towards the shore for flathead and bream. Float fish while using bread for bait in close for mullet and garfish. Work hard bodied lures parallel to the rock wall upstream for bass and TT Switchblades of the small sandy beach for flathead and bream.

BAITS AND LURES

Try those ZMan 3-inch scented Podyz and Minnowz, 4-inch Diezel Minnowz and Swimmerz soft plastics, plus Gulp 4-inch Nemesis and Grubs. Best baits by far are pink nipper and blood worms. You could also try using chicken breast and mullet strips. Green weed for the luderick and bread for the mullet and garfish.

BEST TIDE/TIMES

Run-in or run-out tide for the bream and flathead. Run-up tide for the mullet and garfish. Run-out for the luderick along the rock breakwall downstream of the beach.

AMENITIES

Toilets, covered picnic table BBQ's and plenty of parking.

KIDS AND FAMILIES

Great place to bring family and friends for a fish. You can also kick or throw a ball around or maybe have a game of cricket here when the fish are not biting. Don't forget to bring a picnic and your BBQ tools are there are plenty of places to sit for a while.

POOL FLAT – ROYAL NATIONAL PARK

HOW TO GET THERE 🔍

Whether you are travelling form the north or up from the south along the Prince Highway you will need to turn at the set of lights at Farnell Avenue that leads to the entrance to the Royal National Park. There is a fee to park your car when using the RNP. This can be paid at the shop at Audley. Work your way down the road and you will need to cross the weir at Audley and park in the cark park on the eastern side of the weir. From here you will need to walk back to the weir and take the track out to the area called Pool Flat. It's about a five-minute walk.

ABOVE: *Not only is there a nice retaining wall to fish from the NP have put in a pontoon as well.*

Once you have walked from the parking area near the Audley weir its will just be a matter of picking a spot as to where you would like to fish. The water is fairly-deep along this stretch of shoreline and a descent cast will get you out into where the fish should be feeding. A few years back my son hooked into an Australian salmon, only to have it eaten by a bull shark.

One of the best spots is right up in the northern corner.

TACTICS

Small running ball sinker down onto the bait and a sinker down onto a swivel with a metre leader would be ideal for here.

BAITS AND LURES

Try those ZMan 3-inch scented Podyz and Minnowz, 4-inch Diezel Minnowz and Swimmerz soft plastics, plus Gulp 4-inch Nemesis and Grubs. Best baits by far are pink nipper and blood worms. You could also try using chicken breast and mullet strips. Green weed for the luderick and bread for the mullet and garfish.

BEST TIDE/TIMES

Run-in or run-out tide for the bream and flathead. Run-up tide for the mullet and garfish. Run-out for the luderick along the rock breakwall downstream of the beach.

AMENITIES

There are a couple of tables here. Toilets are back at the Audley Dance Hall Cafe.

KIDS AND FAMILIES

About hallway along there is a wharf and floating pontoon that you can fish from. Remember to take your rubbish with you. Wharf out for the Bundeena Ferry that come along from time to time. Park fee applies if you are going to park your car here.

SNAPSHOT 🔍

Platform
ROCK RETAINING WALLS AND PONTOON

Target species
BREAM
DUSKY FLATHEAD
GARFISH
MULLET

Best baits
HALF PILCHARDS
GARFISH, SQUID,
WORMS PINK NIPPERS,
PRAWNS BREAD
PUDDING BAITS

Best lures
SMALL STICK BAITS &
SURFACE LURES, SOFT
PLASTICS AND VIBES

Best time
RISING AND
FALLING TIDES

SEASONS

Bream **Feb.– May**
Dusky flathead
Year round
Garfish **Year round**
Mullet **Year round**

🔍 HOW TO GET THERE

To gain access to here you will need to enter the RNP at the lights at Farnell Avenue that leads to the entrance to the Royal National Park. Work your way down the road and travel across the weir at Audley, up the hill and continue along St Bertram Stevens Drive until you come to Warumbul Road on your right. This road then leads down towards the water, but take care as the last section of the road is not surfaced.

🔍 SNAPSHOT

Platform
SMALL SANDY BEACH AT LOW TIDE, ROCK RETAINING WALLS

Target species
BREAM
KINGFISH
LEATHERJACKETS
LUDERICK
PANED SIZED SNAPPER
SALMON
SILVER TREVALLY
SQUID
TAILOR

Best baits
HALF PILCHARDS GARFISH. SQUID, WORMS, PINK NIPPERS, PRAWNS, BREAD & PUDDING BAITS

Best lures
SMALL STICK BAITS & SURFACE LURES, SOFT PLASTICS AND VIBES

Best time
RISING AND FALLING TIDES

SEASONS

Bream **Feb.– May**
Kingfish **Nov.– May**
Leatherjackets
Year round
Luderick **Mar.– Sep.**
Pan sized snapper **Winter**
Salmon **Mar.– Jun.**
Silver trevally **Mar.– Jun.**
Squid **Year round**
Tailor **Mar.– Aug.**

ABOVE: *Make sure that you bring some berley along with you when fishing from here as it seems to bring in the big ones.*

LEFT: *The water is fairly deep here and a wide cast will bring you a couple of fish. Nippers are best used here.*

The secluded Warumbul picnic area is an ideal bush getaway with scenic water views across Port Hacking in Royal National Park. While you are down there having a fish, you will be in with a good chance of seeing a deer or two, a few wallabies and plenty of birdlife. Dolphins and turtles frequent this bay during the year. There is a fee to park your car when using the RNP. This can be paid at the shop at Audley.

TACTICS

Kingfish. Salmon and tailor will feed in this bay at times. Try using 40 to 60-gram metal slicers to get that extra distance. When the fish are in closer you could try casting out poppers, shallow hard bodied lures and lightly weighted soft plastics. Suspend either a whole pilchard or garfish underneath a bobby cork.

BAITS AND LURES

Try those ZMan 3-inch scented Podyz and Minnowz, 4-inch Diezel Minnowz and Swimmerz soft plastics, plus Gulp 4-inch Nemesis and Grubs. Best baits by far are pink nipper and blood worms. You could also try using chicken breast and mullet strips. Green weed for the luderick and bread for the mullet and garfish. Take a few metal slicers for the tailor, salmon and kingfish and don't forget the squid jigs.

BEST TIDE/TIMES

Fish out wide when the tide is low and in close when the tide is up. Early morning and late afternoon or on overcast days seems to produce better quality fish.

AMENITIES

Nearby toilets, picnic tables and bike tracks.

KIDS AND FAMILIES

To get to here you will need to take about a 5 to 10-minute walk from the carpark at the Audley Dance Hall Café. You may need to bring some extra chairs and tables. Garbage bins are provided. Park fee applies if you are going to park your car here.

COSTENS POINT TRAIL

HOW TO GET THERE

To gain access to here you will need to enter the RNP at the lights at Farnell Avenue that leads to the entrance to the Royal National Park. Work your way down the road and travel across the weir at Audley, up the hill and continue along St Bertram Stevens Drive until you come to Bundeena Road. Turn right and proceed to Maianbar Road on your right. As you travel along here you will need to keep an eye out for Costens Point Road on your left. This is an unsealed road that you can park at the end and then walk down through the bush to the point.

ABOVE: *Very good deep-water spot. You will need to park your car and walk along the track to get here.*

RIGHT: *Work those diving hard-bodied lures, surface poppers and plastics parallel to the shoreline when fishing here for bream.*

SNAPSHOT

Platform
SANDY BEACH, ROCK RETAINING WALLS

Target species
BREAM
LEATHERJACKETS
LUDERICK
PANED SIZED SNAPPER
SALMON, YELLOWTAIL
SILVER TREVALLY
SQUID, TAILOR

Best baits
HALF PILCHARDS
GARFISH, SQUID,
WORMS, PINK
SNIPPERS BREAD &
PUDDING BAITS

Best lures
SSMALL STICK BAITS &
SURFACE LURES, SOFT
PLASTICS AND VIBES

Best time
RISING AND
FALLING TIDES

SEASONS
Bream **Feb.– May**
Leatherjackets
Year round
Luderick **Mar.– Sep.**
Paned sized snapper **Winter**
Salmon **Mar.– Jun.**
Silver trevally **Mar.– Jun.**
Squid **Year round**
Tailor **Mar.– Aug.**
Tailor **Mar.– Aug**
Yellowtail **Year round**

I f you go by car you will need to park it and walk or ride a mountain bike along the 2.8 kms return fire trail to a small cleared area that is directly beside the Port Hacking River. Along the way, you may come across deer, wombats and other wildlife.

TACTICS

Kingfish. Salmon and tailor will patrol past here at times. Try using 40 to 60-gram metal slicers to get that extra distance. When the fish are in closer you could try casting out poppers, shallow hard bodied lures and lightly weighted soft plastics. Suspend either a whole pilchard or garfish underneath a bobby cork.

BAITS AND LURES

Try those ZMan 3-inch scented Podyz and Minnowz, 4-inch Diezel Minnowz and Swimmerz soft plastics, plus Gulp 4-inch Nemesis and Grubs. Best baits by far are pink nipper and blood worms. You could also try using chicken breast and mullet strips. Green weed for the luderick and bread for the mullet and garfish. Take a few metal slicers for the tailor, salmon and kingfish and don't forget the squid jigs.

BEST TIDE/TIMES

Fish out wide when the tide is low and in close when the tide is up. Early morning and late afternoon or on overcast days seems to produce better quality fish.

AMENITIES

None. Closest toilets are at Warumbul.

KIDS AND FAMILIES

Park fee applies if you are going to park your car here.

MAIANBAR

🔍 HOW TO GET THERE

To gain access to here you will need to enter the RNP at the lights at Farnell Avenue that leads to the entrance to the Royal National Park. Work your way down the road and travel across the weir at Audley, up the hill and continue along St Bertram Stevens Drive until you come to Bundeena Road. Turn right and proceed to Maianbar Road on your right and follow this down to the small hamlet of Maianbar.

🔍 SNAPSHOT

Platform
SANDY BEACH

Target species
BREAM
DUSKY FLATHEAD
SALMON
SILVER TREVALLY
SQUID
TAILOR

Best baits
HALF PILCHARDS, GARFISH, SQUID, WORMS, PINK NIPPERS, PRAWNS, BREAD & PUDDING BAITS

Best lures
SMALL STICK BAITS & SURFACE LURES, SOFT PLASTICS AND VIBES

Best time
RISING AND FALLING TIDES

SEASONS

Bream **Feb.– May**
Dusky flathead
Nov.– Apr.
Salmon **Mar.– Jun.**
Silver trevally
Mar.– Jun.
Squid **Year round**
Tailor **Mar.– Aug.**

ABOVE: *The author pumping a few nippers for his next session at high tide on the flats at Mainbar.*

LEFT: *A couple of hours work fishing with live nippers has produced a few quality fish.*

Maianbar is a village on the outskirts of southern Sydney and is a small hamlet situated in the Royal National Park. There are a couple of small bays, a large sand flat (at low tide), small creek that leads up to Cabbage Tree Basin and a number of walking trails that lead to Bundeena.

TACTICS

Work soft plastics and small diving lures along the edge for flathead, bream and whiting. Float fish with green weed for luderick in the small creek on the western side of the flats. You could also try using small pieces of squid or prawns for leatherjackets.

BAITS AND LURES

When the tide is, high try using surface lures like poppers, stick baits and lightly weighted soft plastics. When the tide is about half way down make your way over to the edge of the sand bar and fish into the deeper water. Pump a few pink nippers nearby. Blood worms are a great bait here.

BEST TIDE/TIMES

If you don't mind getting wet you could work soft plastics, surface lures and small diving hard bodied lures over the flats as the tide falls. Nearby creek is best fished near the top of the tide.

AMENITIES

Nearby café and general store with toilets.

KIDS AND FAMILIES

Small cark park, playground and walking tracks are found at the end of the road.

HOW TO GET THERE

To gain access to here you will need to enter the RNP at the lights at Farnell Avenue that leads to the entrance to the Royal National Park. Work your way down the road and travel across the weir at Audley, up the hill and continue along St Bertram Stevens Drive until you come to Bundeena Road. Turn right and proceed to Maianbar Road on your right and follow this down to the small hamlet of Maianbar. Park your car and walk across the sand flats at low tide to Dee Ban Spit. You do not have to pay a National Park fee to park at Maianbar.

ABOVE: *Two little keen anglers patiently wait for the next bite while fishing off Dee Ban Spit on a run-out tide.*

RIGHT: *You can't get the smile off Riley Brown's face when he catches a whiting while using beach worms for bait.*

SNAPSHOT

Platform
SANDY BEACH

Target species
BREAM
DUSKY FLATHEAD
SALMON
SILVER TREVALLY
SQUID
TAILOR

Best baits
HALF PILCHARDS
GARFISH, SQUID,
WORMS, PINK NIPPERS,
PRAWNS, BREAD &
PUDDING BAITS

Best lures
SMALL STICK BAITS &
SURFACE LURES, SOFT
PLASTICS AND VIBES

Best time:
RISING AND
FALLING TIDES

SEASONS
Bream **Feb.– May**
Dusky flathead
Nov.– Apr.
Salmon **Mar.– Jun.**
Silver trevally **Oct.– Apr.**
Squid **Year round**
Tailor **Mar.– Aug.**

The Dee Ban Spit runs north/south across the main flow of the Port Hacking River and can be accessed by walking from Bundeena west along the beach or coming in from Maianbar. Depending on where you are fishing from the water depth varies from 3 to 9 metres in depth.

TACTICS

Salmon and tailor will school up here feeding on the baitfish, so don't forget those metal slicers, poppers and lightly weighted soft plastics. Either the ball sinkers down onto the hook or the running sinker onto the swivel and a long leader will be the undoing of many a fish.

BAITS AND LURES

Pink nippers and blood worms would be the go-to baits. Try those ZMan 3-inch scented Podyz and Minnowz, 4-inch Diezel Minnowz and Swimmerz soft plastics, plus Gulp 4-inch Nemesis and Grubs. Whole garfish and pilchards on a set of ganged hooks.

BEST TIDE/TIMES

Fish from the eastern side of the spit on the run-out tide into the deep water. When the tide is rising, you can go to the end of the spit or fish for whiting and bream in the small channel behind the spit.

AMENITIES

The closest toilets are either at Maianbar, Bundeena and Bonnie Vale camp grounds.

KIDS AND FAMILIES

Great place to bring the kids for a fish.

CABBAGE TREE BASIN

🔍 HOW TO GET THERE

To gain access to here you will need to enter the RNP at the lights at Farnell Avenue that leads to the entrance to the Royal National Park. Work your way down the road and travel across the weir at Audley, up the hill and continue along St Bertram Stevens Drive until you come to Bundeena Road. Turn right and proceed along this road into the township of Bundeena. Park your car and walk across the sand flats at low tide to Dee Ban Spit. You do not have to pay a National Park fee to park at Maianbar.

🔍 SNAPSHOT

Platform
SANDY BEACH, MANGROVES AND SMALL WALK ACROSS BRIDGE

Target species
BREAM
DUSKY FLATHEAD
MULLET
WHITING

Best baits
HALF PILCHARDS, GARFISH, SQUID, WORMS, PINK NIPPERS, PRAWNS, BREAD & PUDDING BAITS

Best lures
SMALL STICK BAITS & SURFACE LURES, SOFT PLASTICS AND VIBES

Best time
RISING AND FALLING TIDES

SEASONS

Bream **Feb.– May**
Dusky flathead
Year round
Mullet **Year round**
Whiting **Year round**

ABOVE: *The right hand side of the bridge leads to the main river and the left hand side leads to cabbage Tree Basin. The basin can be accessed either side of the low tide*

RIGHT: *Brad Chin managed this lovely luderick while float fishing for*

This is a small deep basin that is up in the back of Bonnie Vale and Maianbar that won't produce a lot of fish, but they are usually quality fish. Access around the shoreline in places can be a bit hard.

TACTICS

Great place to while away the hours watching for the float to go down when fishing for mullet. Work those TT Switchblades and ZMan and Gulp Soft plastics along the shoreline and into the deeper section of the basin. Pink nippers and blood worms would be the go-to baits. Try those ZMan 3-inch scented Podyz and Minnowz, 4-inch Diezel Minnowz and Swimmerz soft plastics, plus Gulp 4-inch Nemesis and Grubs.

BAITS AND LURES

Best fished on the run-out tide.

BEST TIDE/TIMES

You will find that the eastern side of this point is fished the most. Therefore the run-out tide would be the best time to fish from here as your baits and rigs will stay away from the snags that are in close. During the cooler months of the year the luderick will school up here and quite often it can be shoulder-to-shoulder fishing when they're on the chew.

AMENITIES

Closest toilets are at Bonnie Vale, Bundeena and Maianbar.

KIDS AND FAMILIES

There are shops, cafes and a playground at Bundeena, grassed areas with picnic tables and BBQ's at Bonnie Vale and a café at Maianbar.

BUNDEENA

HOW TO GET THERE

To gain access to here you will need to enter the RNP at the lights at Farnell Avenue that leads to the entrance to the Royal National Park. Work your way down the road and travel across the weir at Audley, up the hill and continue along St Bertram Stevens Drive until you come to Bundeena Road. Turn right and proceed along this road into the township of Bundeena. You do not have to pay a National Park fee to park at Bundeena.

ABOVE: *The rocks at Bundenna will produce a good feed on luderick on a falling tide, just remember to have a berley trail going to keep them there.*

LEFT: *Don't forget to have a few Fish Inc squid jigs in your tackle bag as squid are commonly caught here.*

prawns and small pieces of squid in close to the wharf and rocks.

BAITS AND LURES

Soft plastics and blades can be worked from the wharf and adjacent shoreline over the sandy bottom. 30 to 60gram metal slicers for tailor, salmon and kingfish. Also, try using poppers and lightly weighted ZMan 5 and 7-inch scented Jerk ShadZ rigged on TT ChinlockZ weedless jig heads.

BEST TIDE/TIMES

It doesn't seem to matter whether the tide is coming in or going out. Best times are early morning or late afternoons. Another good time would be when the Cronulla ferry has just left the wharf and stirred up the bottom.

AMENITIES

Toilets are in a carpark near the road leading down to the wharf.

KIDS AND FAMILIES

There are a few cafes, restaurant's and a great fish and chip shop not far from the wharf. There is also a playground in the centre of town. On the south-western side of the wharf there is a swimming area and you can also give paddle boarding ago by hiring one from www.bundeenakayaks.com.au/

At Bundeena, you will find a ferry wharf, walkway and plenty of beach that you can fish from. From Bundeena Wharf and to the other side of Cabbage Tree point in the west the shoreline is an IPAs and the collecting of seashore animals is strictly prohibited in these closures. This includes crabs, snails, cunjevoi, octopus, sea urchins, anemones, pipis, cockles, mussels, oysters, and nippers. The area extends from the mean high-water mark to 10 metres seaward from the mean low water mark. Fishing is permitted in these areas, but bait collection is not allowed, although you may bring bait with you up to the quantity allowed by NSW Fisheries.

TACTICS

Try suspending either a whole squid, garfish or pilchard underneath a bobby cork for kingfish, salmon and tailor. Small ball sinker down onto a half pillie tail or strip of squid, tuna or mullet for bream and flathead. Luderick in close to the wharf or rocky shoreline with a stemmed float and either green weed or cabbage. Leatherjackets on peeled

SNAPSHOT

Platform
RETAINING WALLS, FERRY WHARF

Target species
BREAM
KINGFISH, YELLOWTAIL
LEATHERJACKETS
LUDERICK
SALMON, SQUID
SILVER TREVALLY
TAILOR

Best baits
HALF PILCHARDS, GARFISH, SQUID, WORMS, PINK NIPPERS, BREAD & PUDDING BAITS

Best lures
SMALL STICK BAITS & SURFACE LURES, SOFT PLASTICS AND VIBES

Best time
RISING AND FALLING TIDES

SEASONS

Bream **Feb.– May**
Kingfish **Nov.– May**
Leatherjackets
Year round
Luderick **Mar.– Sep.**
Salmon **Mar.– Jun.**
Silver trevally **Mar.– Jun.**
Squid **Year round**
Tailor **Mar.– Aug.**
Yellowtail **Year round**

BUNDEENA POINT

🔍 HOW TO GET THERE

To gain access to here you will need to enter the RNP at the lights at Farnell Avenue that leads to the entrance to the Royal National Park. Work your way down the road and travel across the weir at Audley, up the hill and continue along St Bertram Stevens Drive until you come to Bundeena Road. Turn right and proceed along this road into the township of Bundeena. You do not have to pay a National Park fee to park at Bundeena.

This area of rocks and sandy beach produces squid right though the changing of the tides.

BELOW: *Peeled prawns are the go when fishing from the shote here. Just remember to peel them and use small circle hooks.*

🔍 SNAPSHOT

Platform
ROCKS

Target species
BREAM
DRUMMER
DUSKY FLATHEAD
LEATHERJACKETS
LUDERICK
SQUID
TAILOR

Best baits
HALF PILCHARDS, GARFISH, SQUID, WORMS, PINK NIPPERS, BREAD & PUDDING BAITS

Best lures
SMALL STICK BAITS & SURFACE LURES, SOFT PLASTICS AND VIBES

Best time
RISING AND FALLING TIDES

SEASONS

Bream **Feb.– May**
Drummer **Autumn to the end of winter**
Leatherjackets **Year round**
Luderick **Mar.– Sep.**
Squid **Year round**
Tailor **Dec.– Apr.**

This is a small point that juts out into the entrance to the Port Hacking River. It is a very protected spot to fish in the southerly and northerly wind. Not much chop when there is a westly blowing. When bait fishing here you will always need to have small and steady berley trail. Try using one of those ball throwing devices that you chuck balls for a dog, these are great to get your berley bomb out further into the deeper water.

TACTICS

Try suspending either a whole squid, garfish or pilchard underneath a bobby cork for tailor. Small ball sinker down onto a half pillie tail or strip of squid, tuna or mullet for bream and flathead. Luderick in close to the wharf or rocky shoreline with a stemmed float and either green weed or cabbage. Leatherjackets on peeled prawns and small pieces of squid in close to the wharf and rocks.

BAITS AND LURES

Soft plastics and blades can be worked from the shoreline over the sandy bottom. 30 to 60gram metal slicers for tailor, salmon and kingfish. Also, try using poppers and lightly weighted ZMan 5 and 7-inch scented Jerk ShadZ rigged on TT ChinlockZ weedless jig heads.

BEST TIDE/TIMES

It doesn't seem to matter whether the tide is coming in or going out. Best times are early morning or late afternoons. Another good time would be a couple of days when there have been big seas, as the fish come in here for a bit of a rest.

AMENITIES

Toilets are in a carpark near the road leading down to the wharf.

KIDS AND FAMILIES

There are a few cafes, restaurant's and a great fish and chip shop not far from the wharf. There is also a playground in the centre of town. On the south-western side of the wharf there is a swimming area and you can also give paddle boarding ago by hiring one from www.bundeenakayaks.com.au/

JIBBON BEACH

HOW TO GET THERE

To gain access to here you will need to enter the RNP at the lights at Farnell Avenue that leads to the entrance to the Royal National Park. Work your way down the road and travel across the weir at Audley, up the hill and continue along St Bertram Stevens Drive until you come to Bundeena Road. Turn right and proceed along this road into the township of Bundeena. Turn right at Loftus Street and follow this down to the western end of Jibbon Beach. Park your car and walk down to the beach. You do not have to pay a National Park fee to park at Bundeena.

ABOVE: *Try fishing here is a southerly wind for the best results.*

SNAPSHOT

Platform
SANDY BEACH

Target species
BREAM
FLATHEAD
SALMON
SILVER TREVALLY
TAILOR
SQUID
WHITING

Best baits
HALF PILCHARDS, GARFISH, SQUID, WORMS, PINK NIPPERS, BREAD & PUDDING BAITS

Best lures
SMALL STICK BAITS & SURFACE LURES, SOFT PLASTICS AND VIBES

Best time
RISING AND FALLING TIDES

SEASONS

Bream **Feb.– May**
Sand & Dusky flathead **Nov.– May**
Salmon **Mar.– Jun.**
Silver trevally **Mar.– Jun.**
Squid **Year round**
Tailor **Mar.– Aug.**
Whiting **Year round**

A beautiful sandy beach that runs out to Jibbon Point. Protected from and southerly winds and a nor'easter.

TACTICS

This is predominately a bream, whiting and flathead beach throughout the year. Great place to give those squid jigs that you have lying around. Salmon and tailor can be found feeding on bait school off the beach.

BAITS AND LURES

Pink Nipper, blood and beach worms are by far the best baits. You could also try using half pillies and strips of chicken breast or mullet. Not a bad place to try a few soft plastics and blades. Don't forget the squid jigs.

BEST TIDE/TIMES

Last couple of hours of the rising tide and about two to three hours of the falling tide.

AMENITIES

Closest toilets are back at Bundeena.

KIDS AND FAMILIES

Walk the beach, do a bit of bush walking out to the coast or talk a walk out to the aboriginal carving on the point.

JIBBON POINT

🔍 HOW TO GET THERE

To gain access to here you will need to enter the RNP at the lights at Farnell Avenue that leads to the entrance to the Royal National Park. Work your way down the road and travel across the weir at Audley, up the hill and continue along St Bertram Stevens Drive until you come to Bundeena Road. Turn right and proceed along this road into the township of Bundeena. Turn right at Loftus Street and follow this down to the western end of Jibbon Beach. Park your car and walk down to the beach. You do not have to pay a National Park fee to park at Bundeena.

🔍 SNAPSHOT

Platform
OCEAN ROCKS

Target species
BREAM, DRUMMER GROPER, KINGFISH LEATHERJACKETS LUDERICK, SALMON PANNED SIZED SNAPPER SILVER TREVALLY SQUID, TAILOR TARWHINE, YELLOWTAIL

Best baits
HALF PILCHARDS, GARFISH, SQUID, WORMS, PINK NIPPERS, PRAWNS, BREAD & PUDDING BAITS

Best lures
SMALL STICK BAITS & SURFACE LURES, SOFT PLASTICS AND VIBES

Best time
RISING AND FALLING TIDES

SEASONS
Bream **Feb.– May**
Drummer **Autumn to the end of winter**
Groper **Apr.– Sep.**
Kingfish **Nov.– May**
Leatherjackets **Year round**
Paned sized snapper **Winter**
Salmon **Mar.– Jun.**
Silver trevally **Mar.– Jun.**
Squid **Year round**
Tailor **Mar.– Aug.**
Tarwhine **Feb.– May**
Yellowtail **Year round**

ABOVE: You don't need much tackle when targeting bream and drummer off the rocks.

RIGHT: Scotty Lyons with a couple of large drummer that were caught while using peeled blue-tailed prawns for bait and bread for berley.

A walk with a fishing rod in your hand is an enjoyable way of exploring Jibbon Head and its beaches. From the township on Bundeena, walk through the streets and then along the beautiful Jibbon Beach. At the northern end of Jibbon Beach, a track leads through the bush to an Aboriginal engraving site, then to the point of Jibbon Head. You will enjoy many grand water vistas across Port Hacking along this stretch. From the point, the walk heads along the eastern coastline to Shelley Beach before leading you back through the bush to Jibbon Beach, and then retracing your steps back to Bundeena.

TACTICS
Due to the snaggy bottom, it would be best if you fish with either a small bobby cork or a stem float. As this will keep your bait off the bottom. You could also try using a small (000, 00) ball sinker directly down onto the bait. Making sure that you stay in contact with the bait at all times.

When the seas are up and the swell comes into this small bay you will find that the tailor and salmon sometime move in. Either use a larger bobby cork and suspend a whole pilchard or garfish underneath. You could also try using a lightly weighted pilchard or garfish on a set of ganged hooks. Drummer, bream, trevally and tarwhine respond well to bread for berley and bait. You could also try cunje.

BAITS AND LURES
Pink nippers, peeled prawns, pudding baits, pillie tails or strips of mullet and tuna. Whole pilchards and garfish for the tailor and salmon. 40 to 80-gram metal slicers are always handy to have on hand, as you can get more distance when the fish are out wide.

BEST TIDE/TIMES
Close toilets, cafes and playgrounds are back in Bundeena.

AMENITIES
At this beach you will find great facilities including toilets, showers, change rooms and bubblers, BBQs and a small playground. There are nearby shops that you can get a drink or a feed at.

KIDS AND FAMILIES
Maybe you could do a bit of rock pool exploring with the kids. Make sure you keep an eye out for blue ringed octopus.

WATTAMOLLA BEACH

HOW TO GET THERE

To gain access to here you will need to enter the RNP at the lights at Farnell Avenue that leads to the entrance to the Royal National Park. Work your way down the road and travel across the weir at Audley, up the hill and continue along St Bertram Stevens Drive until you come to Wattamolla Road. Travel along this road until you reach the carpark at the top picnic area.

ABOVE: *If you are going to try for drummer and bream, here try pumping nippers at Maianbar before you go.*

RIGHT: *Gary and Marcus looking for a couple of beach worms and maybe the odd pipi or two.*

SNAPSHOT

Platform
SANDY BEACH

Target species
BREAM
SALMON
SILVER TREVALLY
TAILOR
TARWHINE
WHITING

Best baits
HALF PILCHARDS,
GARFISH, SQUID,
WORMS, PINK NIPPERS,
PRAWNS, BREAD &
PUDDING BAITS

Best lures
SMALL STICK BAITS &
SURFACE LURES, SOFT
PLASTICS AND VIBES

Best time
RISING AND
FALLING TIDES

SEASONS

Bream **Feb.– May**
Dart **Year round**
Salmon **Mar.– Jun.**
Silver trevally **Mar– Jun.**
Tailor **Mar.– Aug.**
Whiting **Year round**

The coastal Wattamolla picnic area at Royal National Park is a popular family spot for swimming, fishing, snorkelling and bushwalking. You may see an eagle or an oyster catcher flying about. So, keep an eye out for them. Deer and wallabies frequent here in the mornings and afternoons.

TACTICS

Whole pilchards and garfish on ganged hooks spun in the surf at each end of the beach can produce tailor and salmon. Lightly weighted half pillies and strip of mullet for the bream and pink nippers and blood worms for the whiting and dart.

BAITS AND LURES

Beach and blood worms, pink nippers, strips of squid, half and whole pillies and garfish. You could also try some salted pipis.

BEST TIDE/TIMES

Anytime other than when a southerly wind is blowing. It can get quite rough here so keep an eye on the swell.

AMENITIES

Toilets, picnic area and a grassed are back up near the top cark park.

KIDS AND FAMILIES

Park fee applies if you are going to park your car here.

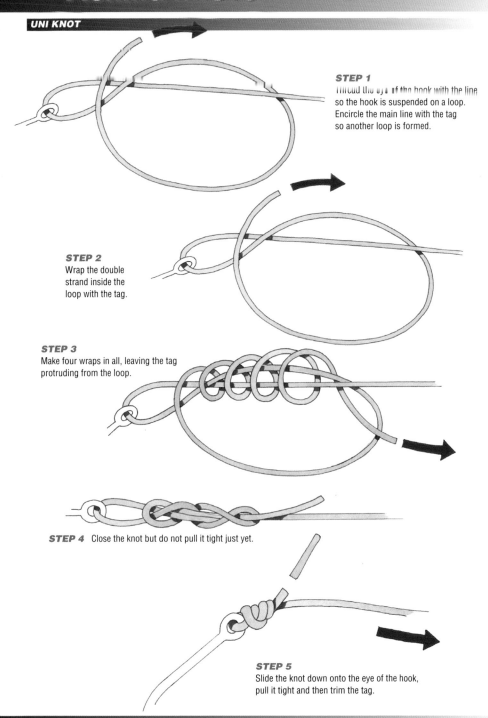

UNI KNOT

STEP 1
Thread the eye of the hook with the line so the hook is suspended on a loop. Encircle the main line with the tag so another loop is formed.

STEP 2
Wrap the double strand inside the loop with the tag.

STEP 3
Make four wraps in all, leaving the tag protruding from the loop.

STEP 4 Close the knot but do not pull it tight just yet.

STEP 5
Slide the knot down onto the eye of the hook, pull it tight and then trim the tag.

DOUBLE UNI KNOT

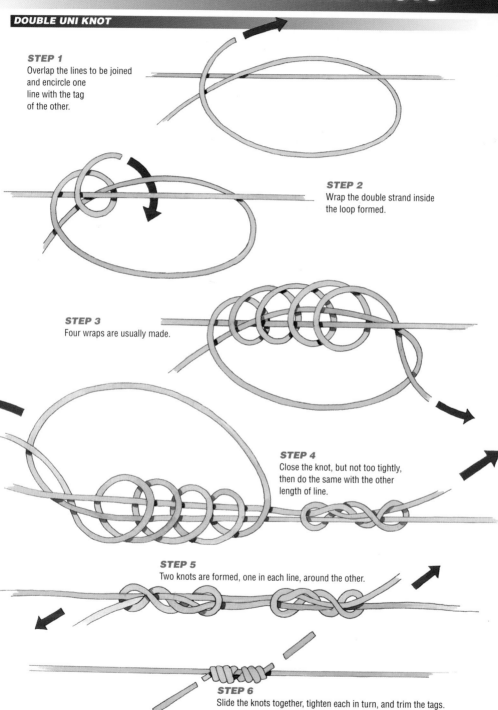

STEP 1
Overlap the lines to be joined and encircle one line with the tag of the other.

STEP 2
Wrap the double strand inside the loop formed.

STEP 3
Four wraps are usually made.

STEP 4
Close the knot, but not too tightly, then do the same with the other length of line.

STEP 5
Two knots are formed, one in each line, around the other.

STEP 6
Slide the knots together, tighten each in turn, and trim the tags.

FISHING KNOTS

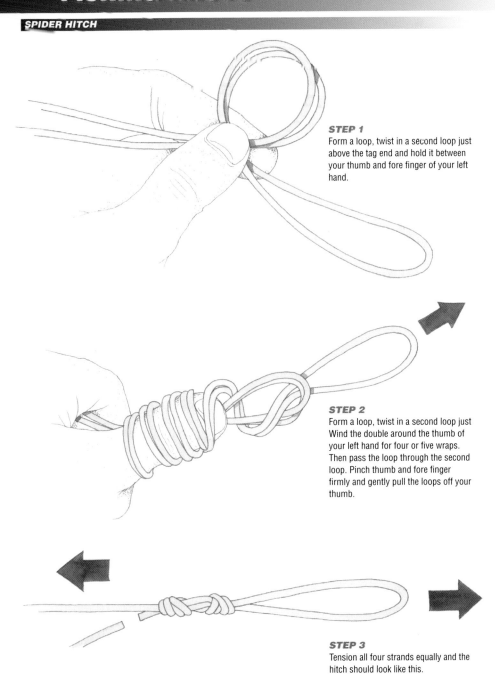

STEP 1
Form a loop, twist in a second loop just above the tag end and hold it between your thumb and fore finger of your left hand.

STEP 2
Form a loop, twist in a second loop just Wind the double around the thumb of your left hand for four or five wraps. Then pass the loop through the second loop. Pinch thumb and fore finger firmly and gently pull the loops off your thumb.

STEP 3
Tension all four strands equally and the hitch should look like this.

🔍 FLOATING LIVE BAIT

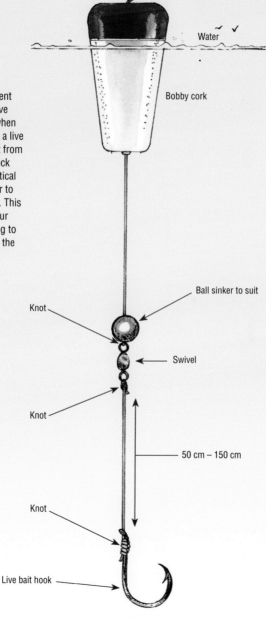

2 x Plastic float stoppers

Main line

Water

Bobby cork

Ball sinker to suit

Knot

Swivel

Knot

50 cm – 150 cm

Knot

Live bait hook

There is often a requirement to position a live bait above the bottom: this occurs when there is a need to present a live bait naturally or to keep it from swimming into bottom rock and weed. The most practical way to fish a live bait near to surface is beneath a float. This rig will satisfy most of your requirements when aiming to present a live bait near to the surface.

PATERNOSTER RIG FOR ESTUARY, ROCK & BEACH

The paternoster rig is used widely in fishing circles. The reason for this is that it is an effective rig for presenting a bait immediately above the bottom. In the event that the bottom provides weed and rock snags, the paternoster rig will enable you to keep a bait above such threats. Waters that offer current such as those in the beach environment are often best fished using a paternoster rig.

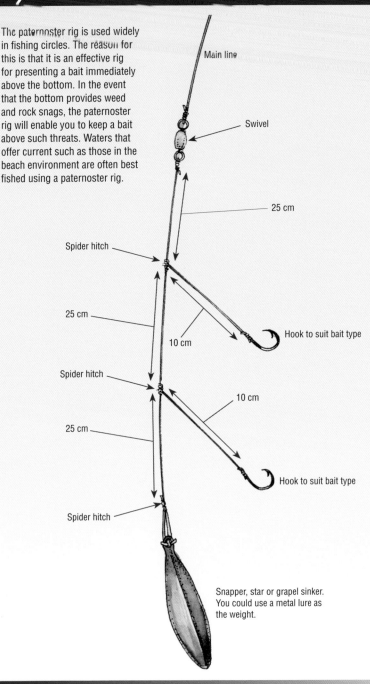

Main line

Swivel

25 cm

Spider hitch

25 cm

10 cm

Hook to suit bait type

Spider hitch

10 cm

25 cm

Hook to suit bait type

Spider hitch

Snapper, star or grapel sinker. You could use a metal lure as the weight.

A running rig is one of the simplest rigs to produce but is often very snag-resistant and deadly on fish. The ability for a fish to 'run' with a bait without feeling too much resistance will often fool cautious feeders. The impact of running a sinker immediately on top of the hook reduces the potential for snagging of the rig. Use just enough weight to get your bait to the depth of the fish and you will be catching them in no time.

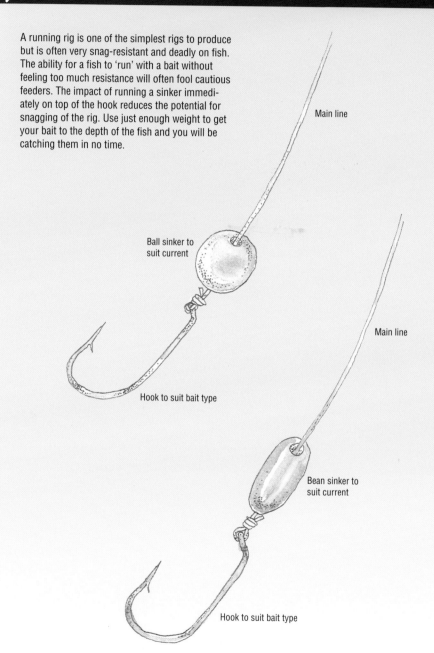

Main line

Ball sinker to suit current

Hook to suit bait type

Main line

Bean sinker to suit current

Hook to suit bait type

BAIT PRESENTATION

SLIDING SNOOD FOR STRIP BAIT

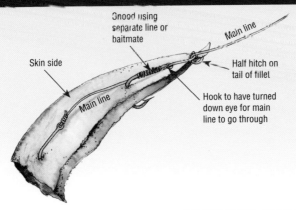

Snood using separate line or baitmate

Main line

Skin side

Main line

Half hitch on tail of fillet

Hook to have turned down eye for main line to go through

SLIDING SNOOD FOR LIVE BAIT

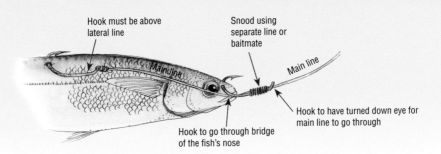

Hook must be above lateral line

Snood using separate line or baitmate

Main line

Main line

Hook to have turned down eye for main line to go through

Hook to go through bridge of the fish's nose

WORMS 1

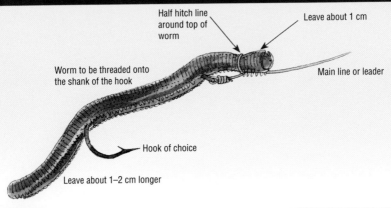

Half hitch line around top of worm

Leave about 1 cm

Worm to be threaded onto the shank of the hook

Main line or leader

Hook of choice

Leave about 1–2 cm longer

BAIT PRESENTATION

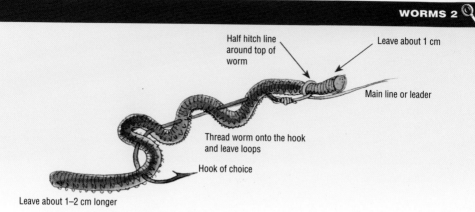

Half hitch line around top of worm

Leave about 1 cm

Main line or leader

Thread worm onto the hook and leave loops

Hook of choice

Leave about 1–2 cm longer

Snood or baitmate

Main line

Turned down eye

Live bait hooks

Main line

Live bait hook

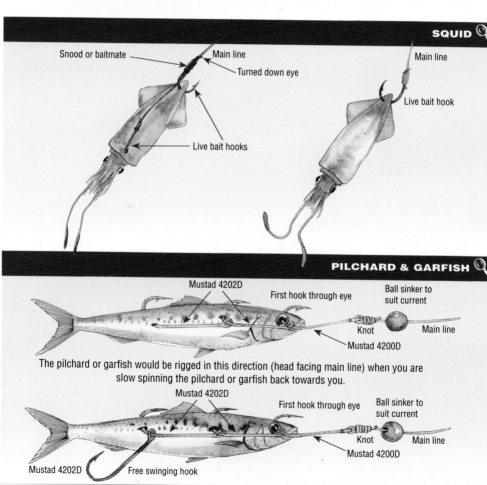

Mustad 4202D

First hook through eye

Ball sinker to suit current

Knot

Main line

Mustad 4200D

The pilchard or garfish would be rigged in this direction (head facing main line) when you are slow spinning the pilchard or garfish back towards you.

Mustad 4202D

First hook through eye

Ball sinker to suit current

Knot

Main line

Mustad 4200D

Mustad 4202D

Free swinging hook

TARGET FISH ID

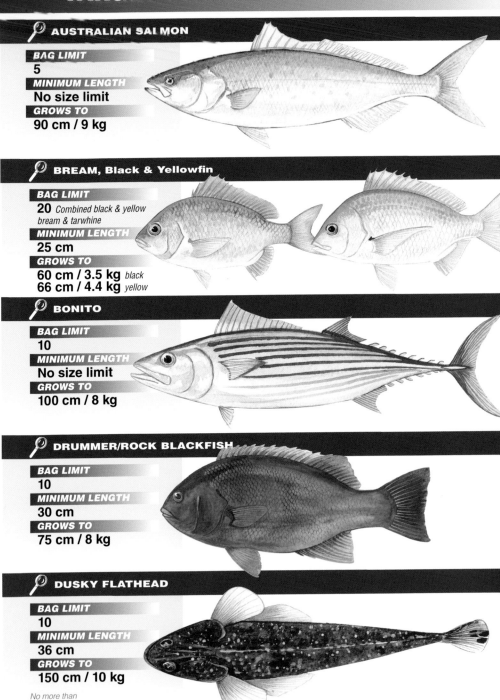

AUSTRALIAN SALMON

BAG LIMIT
5
MINIMUM LENGTH
No size limit
GROWS TO
90 cm / 9 kg

BREAM, Black & Yellowfin

BAG LIMIT
20 Combined black & yellow
bream & tarwhine
MINIMUM LENGTH
25 cm
GROWS TO
60 cm / 3.5 kg black
66 cm / 4.4 kg yellow

BONITO

BAG LIMIT
10
MINIMUM LENGTH
No size limit
GROWS TO
100 cm / 8 kg

DRUMMER/ROCK BLACKFISH

BAG LIMIT
10
MINIMUM LENGTH
30 cm
GROWS TO
75 cm / 8 kg

DUSKY FLATHEAD

BAG LIMIT
10
MINIMUM LENGTH
36 cm
GROWS TO
150 cm / 10 kg

*No more than
1 fish over 70 cm.*

FLOUNDER

BAG LIMIT
20 *Total for all species including sole*

MINIMUM LENGTH
25 cm *No size limit for sole*

GROWS TO
50 cm / 1 kg

GARFISH

BAG LIMIT
20

MINIMUM LENGTH
No size limit

GROPER, Blue, Brown, Red

BAG LIMIT
2 *Only 1 over 60 cm*

MINIMUM LENGTH
30 cm

GROWS TO
120 cm / 30 kg

LEATHERJACKETS

BAG LIMIT
20 *Total for all leatherjackets*

MINIMUM LENGTH
No size limit

GROWS TO
35 cm

LUDERICK

BAG LIMIT
20 *Total for all leatherjackets*

MINIMUM LENGTH
27 cm

GROWS TO
70 cm / 4.5 kg

TARGET FISH ID

KINGFISH

BAG LIMIT
5
MINIMUM LENGTH
65 cm
GROWS TO
150 cm / 65 kg

MACKEREL, SLIMY

BAG LIMIT
50
MINIMUM LENGTH
No size limit
GROWS TO
50 cm / 2 kg

MULLET, SEA

BAG LIMIT
20 *Combined take*
MINIMUM LENGTH
30 cm *Max. 15 cm live bait*
GROWS TO
80 cm / 5 kg

MULLOWAY

BAG LIMIT
5
MINIMUM LENGTH
45 cm
GROWS TO
180 cm / 60 kg

*No more than
2 fish over 70 cm.*

SAND WHITING

BAG LIMIT
20 *Combined total of all whiting*
MINIMUM LENGTH
27 cm *Sand whting only*
GROWS TO
47 cm / 1 kg

TARGET FISH ID

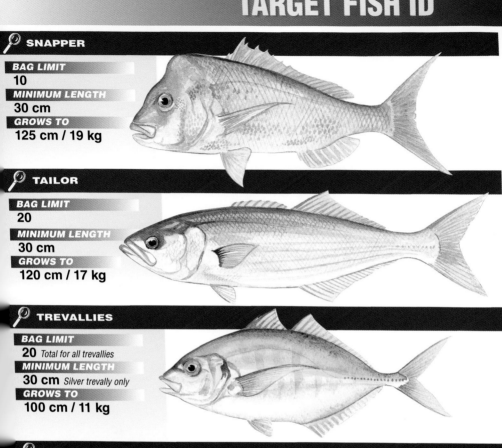

SNAPPER

BAG LIMIT
10
MINIMUM LENGTH
30 cm
GROWS TO
125 cm / 19 kg

TAILOR

BAG LIMIT
20
MINIMUM LENGTH
30 cm
GROWS TO
120 cm / 17 kg

TREVALLIES

BAG LIMIT
20 Total for all trevallies
MINIMUM LENGTH
30 cm Silver trevally only
GROWS TO
100 cm / 11 kg

YELLOWTAIL

BAG LIMIT
50
MINIMUM LENGTH
No size limit
GROWS TO
50 cm / 1.5 kg

BEACH WORMS

BAG LIMIT
20
MINIMUM LENGTH
No size limit

Whole or in part total 20. All other worms 100 combined total.

SQUID

BAG LIMIT
20

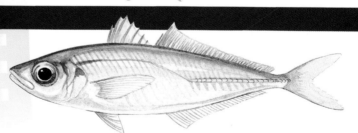

🔍 AUSTRALIAN BASS

BAG LIMIT

2 *(4 possession) combined bass/estuary perch; only 1 (inc. 1 possession) over 35 cm in rivers*

GROWS TO

65 cm / 4 kg

Possession limit 1 over **35 cm** *in rivers*

Bass closed season 1 June – 31 August (rivers/estuary)

🔍 PERCH, ESTUARY

BAG LIMIT

2 *(4 possession) combined bass/estuary perch; only 1 (inc. 1 possession) over 35 cm in rivers*

GROWS TO

65 cm / 7.5 kg

Only 1 over **35 cm** *in rivers*

🔍 PERCH, GOLDEN

BAG LIMIT

5 *Daily (10 possession)*

MINIMUM LENGTH

30 cm

GROWS TO

70 cm / 15 kg

🔍 PERCH, SILVER

BAG LIMIT

5 *in listed dams*

MINIMUM LENGTH

25 cm

GROWS TO

60 cm / 8 kg

(10 possession in listed dams)
NO TAKE RIVERS

🔍 REDFIN

BAG LIMIT

No bag limit

MINIMUM LENGTH

No size limit

FISH COOLER DELUXE RANGE

Keep your catch
ICE COOL for LONGER

Small	915 mm x 460 mm x 300 mm	AC1136
Medium	1220 mm x 510 mm x 300 mm	AC1143
Large	1520 mm x 510 mm x 300 mm	AC1150
Extra Large	1830 mm x 510 mm x 300 mm	AC1167

Small

Medium

Large

Extra Large

KAYAK COOLER DELUXE RANGE

Medium	610 mm length - Top width 180mm - Bottom width x 400 mm	AC1112-11000
Large	910 mm length - Top width 250mm - Bottom width x 510 mm	AC1129-13700

Medium
With rubber handle

Large
With 3 rubber handles